D1393701

Eric A. Rolls Asprey, 1902-
Chairman 1973-9

Asprey
of Bond Street
1781–1981

Bevis Hillier

Quartet Books

London   Melbourne   New York

First published by Quartet Books Limited 1981
A member of the Namara Group
27 Goodge Street, London W1P 1FD
Copyright © Bevis Hillier 1981
ISBN 0 7043 2313 3

Designed by Namara Features
Origination by Waterden Reproductions
Printed in Great Britain by Shenval '80'

Contents

Introduction

The official histories of famous companies and stores fall into two categories. One is the inward-looking kind, which doggedly follows the internal chronology of the firm: 'In 1956, after almost fifty years of sterling service, Mr J.E. Snaith retired as Chief Buyer in the Flatware Department, and was succeeded by Mr E.G.R. Podd, formerly Deputy Buyer in the Small Goods Department.' The only people in the world likely to be interested in such a statement are Mr Snaith, Mr Podd and their loving families.

The other kind of history is in the outward-looking style, where the official historian has frankly recognized that little in the company's history is of the remotest interest to the public. His ingenious method of solving this difficulty is to relate the firm to English history in general, and in particular to any historical event that occurred within either a half-mile radius of the firm's premises or fifty years of its foundation: 'It was only two hundred yards from the present site of the business, and only fourteen years before it was founded, that Lord Mulberry, the Regency rake, who customarily wore Hessian boots and carried an ebony cane, was challenged to a duel by the Hon. Marmaduke Hornbeam, whom he had accused of cheating in a game of piquet at nearby Crockford's.' These confections of picturesque irrelevance are full of broughams, phaetons, periwigs, snuff, quizzing-glasses and bow-fronted windows.

Though two such treatments are of polar dissimilarity, they usually have one thing in common. Both give a big pat on the back to the company they are celebrating (and which is paying them).

The House of X is a London landmark, a rambling four-storey slice of British tradition standing on half an acre of golden real estate in the heart of the West End. The name of X has passed

Mr P. F. Hubbard

into the language as a symbol of quality. It has been a byword in the world of luxury goods for the past two centuries. The dynasty of X, moving in unbroken line from father to son, has lived through the reigns of six monarchs, many of whom have honoured X's with a 'By Royal Appointment' sign. A veritable Aladdin's cave, X's has become a required stop on the tourist's itinerary, like the Tower of London or Madame Tussaud's. Yet the invitation it extends to the visitor is a discreet one. It does not inveigle with garish signs or neon lighting. Once inside, you are cocooned in a womb of luxury, a refuge from the hurly-burly, where all is serene and assured. You are as welcome whether you come to spend thousands or just to browse. No service is too great – or too small – for the staff. Tradition has been staunchly upheld; but X's has not lagged behind in fashion. Its vitality is as enduring as its quality...

All this must be very gratifying to the latest Mr X and his heirs, but it can hardly be classed as history.

The chronicler of Asprey's may not be able to avoid these pitfalls entirely, but there are several mitigating circumstances. First, the internal history of the company is far from dull. Even its beginnings among the lavender fields of Mitcham are unorthodox. The staff, and the manufacturers who supplied the shop, have not been just a succession of amiable non-entities. The manufacturers have included Ernest Betjemann[1], the Chippendale of the twentieth century, whose son happens to be the Poet Laureate, Sir John Betjeman. Until only two years ago, the staff included Mr P.F. Hubbard, who had been working at Asprey's since 1905 – the year before Sir John was born. Asprey's have been in Bond Street since 1841, and Mr Hubbard had been a witness to the company's history for more than half that period of 140 years. He remembered the funeral of King Edward VII, and in 1969 King Edward's great-grand-daughter, the present Queen, created him a Member of the Royal Victorian Order in recognition of his unique record of service – an honour which lies within the direct gift of the sovereign and is not conferred on the recommendation of the Prime Minister.

As for the pat on the back, all the things in my spoof paragraph are true of Asprey's, but if a shop is really a byword and a household name it must be superfluous to say so.

The Mitcham Origins

Asprey's beginnings were modest. Writing about the firm in *The Times* (1971), Philip Howard was surprised to learn that 'The home of luxury and inset ivory backgammon tables started, improbably, in Mitcham. William Asprey, descended from a family of Huguenots who had escaped from France, founded the firm there in 1781.'

Mitcham today certainly has little in common with Bond Street. Sir Nikolaus Pevsner and Ian Nairn describe it as 'the epitome of London-over-the-border – an indescribable mess'. But the genius of the place survived Mitcham's transmogrification into an Art-Deco and mock-Tudor suburb of London. What Lieutenant-Colonel H.F. Bidder, then the unofficial 'squire' of Mitcham, wrote in a commemorative booklet of 1923 holds good today: 'There still exists, embedded in and affecting this great community, the strong and wholesome organism of a Surrey village.'

Mitcham was best known for its lavender. An old children's rhyme ran:

> Sutton for mutton,
> Kirby for beef,
> Mitcham for lavender
> And Dartford for a thief.

However, camomile was the main crop, and other herbs grown commercially included peppermint, liquorice, Provence roses for rose-water, damask roses – plucked in bud – for *pot-pourri*, belladonna, marsh malop, pennyroyal and the sinister 'squirting cucumber' (*mormordica*), from which elaterium was extracted, which had to be picked by men in masks because of the acrid, blistering spray ejected when it was plucked.

Mitcham was said to be the most fragrant village in England, but away from the mingled scents of the herbs which kept most of the pharmacies of London supplied with drugs, another industry flourished in the late eighteenth century: calico and silk printing. The River Wandle was so infested with mills that it was described as 'the hardest worked river of its size in the realm'. Calico had to be bleached before it was printed and the cloth was spread out in the low-lying water meadows of the Wandle for this purpose. The calico and silk printers were mostly of Huguenot stock; in the late sixteenth century Ravensbury Manor, Mitcham, was occupied by Sir Nicholas Throgmorton, a Protestant who supported the Huguenot cause and may have helped refugees from France to settle in the Wandle valley. In 1117 a community of Augustinian canons had been founded at Merton Priory by Gilbert Norman, Sheriff of Surrey, and Thomas a Becket was educated there under the first Prior. When the Priory was advertised to let in 1680, calico printers and manufacturers of felt and beaver hats established themselves on the site. By 1714 a wealthy Huguenot calico printer called Mauvillain, living in a house called 'Growtes' near Morden Lodge in Morden Hall Park, employed 250 men in his factories at Wandsworth and Mitcham. Other Huguenots in the area included the Dubois family, the de St Lays of Collier's Wood, and Peter Waldo of The Elms, Mitcham.

In 1944 when Mr A.T. Butler, Windsor Herald, was doing some genealogical research on behalf of Mr Eric Asprey, he traced a William Asprey, calico printer of Merton; in 1756 William made a deposition identifying the handwriting (in her will) of Anastasia, Dowager Countess of Peterborough, who had lived at Turvey, some four miles due east of Olney, Bucks. This strongly suggests a family connection between the Aspreys of Merton and Mitcham, calico printers, and the Aspreys of Olney, hemp-dressers and 'lace-men', neighbours of the poet William Cowper in whose letters they are mentioned. The Aspreys of Olney were militant Protestants, as might be expected of a Huguenot family, and as practising Non-conformists they fell foul of the law. At the Quarter Sessions of July 1684 Samuel Asprey of Olney, hemp-dresser, was indicted for riot and unlawful assembly with his brother John (also a hemp-dresser) and his sister-in-law Elizabeth, wife of his brother Thomas. By William and Mary's Toleration Act of 1689, Protestant dissenters were allowed to build conventicles and, on registration, to worship

Asprey's Family Tree

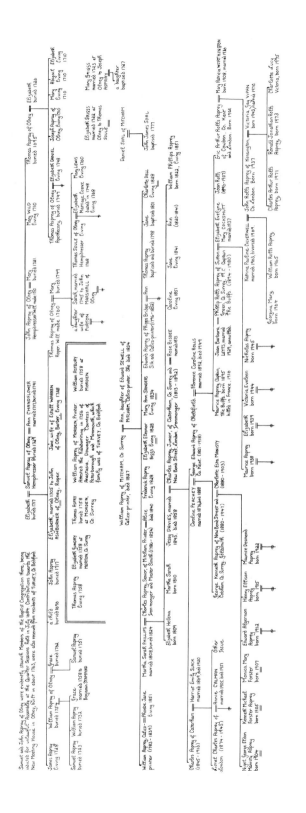

Note that the family name appeared in several variant spellings until the nineteenth century, when it was standardized as Asprey

Charles Asprey, 1813-92

Charles Asprey, 1845-1916

there as they pleased. At the Midsummer Sessions of 1707, the house of John Asprey in Olney was registered as a Public Meeting House. His elder brother Samuel took the Oath of Allegiance in 1723, as did Samuel's son William.

We know that the William Asprey who founded the family business in 1781, grandfather of the Charles Asprey who moved the firm to Bond Street, was buried in Mitcham in June 1827, aged sixty-eight. This means he was probably born in 1759 and could therefore have been the son of Thomas Asprey of Morden who married Elizabeth Gundry of Merton in 1758 – who may in turn have been the son of William Asprey of Olney (d.1754) or his brother Thomas (d.1760).

William Asprey of Mitcham (c.1759-1827) married Ann, daughter of Edward Sewell of Mitcham, who held a copyhold estate in the manor of Biggin and Tamworth, Mitcham. Some of their large family continued the tradition of calico and silk printing. The eldest son William (c.1783-1839) was a calico printer who later moved to Wallington. A younger brother Edward (1796-1852) ran a silk printing works at Phipps Bridge[2], Mitcham, of which Benjamin Slater (writing in 1911 of the factories which printed calico, silk and paisley shawls in his youth, some fifty years earlier) said:

> [there] was a silk printing factory at Phipps Bridge belonging to a Mr *Aspery* [sic], and adjoining this was a large Stocking factory, employing a large number of hands, mostly *Women*; this was burned down and never rebuilt. Next I come to Litler's silk printing Factory, close to Merton Abbey; this factory is still working. I think it is the only one left that carries on the work in Mitcham now.

Benjamin Slater was recording the last stages in the decline of the textile printing industry – a process which was already under way in the late eighteenth century when William Asprey thought it wise to 'diversify' into dressing cases. Miss Bartley of Mitcham Village Green, contributing to the same 1923 booklet as Benjamin Slater, suggested that calico printing went out of fashion in the neo-classical period at the end of the eighteenth century and during the Regency, when the taste was for plainer fabrics. Miss Bartley's memories went back a long way. Her father, a Mitcham doctor, used to chat with Lord

George Edward Asprey,
1851-1918
Chairman 1909-18

Lionel Charles Asprey,
1874-1943
Chairman 1918-22

Nelson when Nelson, living in retirement at Merton, strolled over to Mitcham to watch cricket on the green. 'As my father said to Lord Nelson' was a favourite conversational gambit of hers.

New industries came to Mitcham with the opening, by 1803, of the Surrey Iron Railway, an early English tramway. Coal, flowers and vegetables were transported, and by the end of the nineteenth century glass from Mizen's Glass House had superseded herbs as Mitcham's main product. Pain's Fireworks came to Mitcham in 1876, and by 1926 occupied a dozen acres and employed about two hundred people – occasionally reduced in numbers by spectacular accidents!

The trades chosen by William Asprey's son Charles and grandson Charles – those of ironmonger and smith – were more appropriate to the new industrial Mitcham than was the old Huguenot trade of textile printing which now (at least as it was practised in the Wandle valley) had the standing of a picturesque but archaic handicraft. The old style of textile printing was briefly and magnificently revived at Merton Abbey by William Morris and Company in 1881, and Liberty's continued the traditional Wandle industry for a time.

Charles Asprey I (1786-1854) became a master ironmonger and smith. From 1823 to 1829 he is listed in *Pigot's Commercial Directory* as 'Brazier and tinman' of Mitcham; in 1832 he appears as 'Ironmonger and Smith (furnishing and general)' and by 1839 his son Charles, then twenty-six, must have joined him in the business as *Pigot's Directory* lists 'Asprey & Son, Ironmonger & Smith'. By 1841 Charles Asprey I had amassed enough capital to take the adventurous step of going into partnership with the high-class stationer Francis Kennedy at 49 New Bond Street. Kennedy had originally run his business from 125 Fetter Lane and later from 27 King Street, Holborn, and is first mentioned in the London directories in 1805. Charles Asprey II (1813-92) joined his father in London in 1846, the year after the birth of *his* son Charles Asprey III (1845-1916), the next heir to the business. They moved to 166 New Bond Street in 1847.

George Kenneth Asprey
1880-1947
Chairman 1922-41

Philip Rolls Asprey
1894-1980
Chairman 1941-72

The Rise
of
Bond Street

Bond Street was – and is – the most fashionable street in London, the 'High Street of Mayfair'. Old Bond Street was built in 1686, New Bond Street (as far as Clifford Street) soon after 1700, and the extension to Oxford Street was begun about 1721. The street takes its name from Sir Thomas Bond, its first developer, a tycoon from the south-eastern suburb of Peckham who became Comptroller of the Household to the Queen Mother (Henrietta Maria) and a favourite of James II whom he followed into exile. Bond bought the great Clarendon House and grounds which the historian of the Civil War had built on the north side of Piccadilly, on a plot granted him by Charles II after the Restoration. The name was perpetuated in the Clarendon Hotel, which was almost adjacent to Asprey's until its demolition in 1870; the earliest surviving advertisement for the firm gives the address as 'Charles Asprey, 166 Bond Street, near the Clarendon Hotel'. John Evelyn, who had helped Clarendon lay out his famous gardens and so resented Bond's speculative development, wrote of 'Clarendon House, built by Mr Pratt, since quite demolished by Sir Thomas Bond, &c., who purchased it to build a streete of tenements to his undoing .'

Some writers were inclined to agree with Evelyn and dismiss Bond as a jerry-builder. *A New Critical Review of the Public Buildings of London* (1786) suggested that: 'There is nothing in the whole prodigious length of the two Bond Streets or in any of the adjacent places, though almost all erected within our memories, that has anything worth our attention; several little wretched attempts there are at foppery in building, but they are too inconsiderable even for censure.' But in Fielding's *Tom Jones* (1749) Bond Street, in which part of the action takes place, is described as 'a very good part of town'.

We already encounter a class of fashionable persons known as 'Bond Street loungers' in the *Weekly Journal* of 1 June 1717. However, the renown of Bond Street as a centre of fashion really began when the celebrated Duchess of Devonshire, offended with the inhabitants of Tavistock Street, Covent Garden (the previous fashion centre) because most of them had voted against Fox, drew off the people of rank and led them to Bond Street. The Bond Street loungers had their own way of walking and of wearing their outlandish clothes. George Colman the Younger put them on the stage in his *Heir-at-Law*, first acted in 1797:

> *Lord Duberly:* But why don't you stand up? The boy rolls about like a porpoise in a storm.
> *Dick Dowlas:* That's the fashion, father; that's modern ease. A young fellow is nothing now without the Bond Street roll, a toothpick between his teeth, and his knuckles cramm'd into his coat-pocket. Then away you go, lounging lazily along.

Pennant remarked in 1805 that if the builder of Bond Street could have foreseen the extreme fashion in store for it, he would have made it wider. 'But this', he philosophizes, 'is a fortunate circumstance for the Bond Street loungers, who thus get a nearer glimpse of the fashionable and generally titled ladies that pass and repass from two to five o'clock.' The opening of Regent Street in the Regency period enticed some of the loungers away, but Bond Street remained the correct place for putting in a morning appearance in the West End during the London Season. The first Lord Lytton wrote in his satirical poem of 1831, *The Siamese Twins*:

> And now our Brothers Bond Street enter,
> Dear Street, of London's charms the centre,
> Dear Street! where at a certain hour
> Man's follies bud forth into flower!
> Where the gay minor sighs for fashion;
> Where majors live that minors cash on;
> Where each who wills may suit his wish,
> Here choose a Guido – there his fish.

As the last line suggests, the Bond Street shops offered the widest range of goods for the fashionable to buy, from valuable paintings to codfish. In the same year as Lytton's poem was published, Benjamin Robert Haydon's picture of 'Napoleon at St Helena', painted for Sir Robert Peel, was exhibited at 21 New Bond Street, inspiring a Wordsworth sonnet. The Arundel Society was founded in 1848 at 24 Old Bond Street, formerly Sir Thomas Lawrence's house. It was named after Thomas Howard, Earl of Arundel in the reigns of James I and Charles I, 'the founder of *vertu* in England and the Maecenas of all politer arts'. The Society published essays on arts subjects and chromolithographs of works of art. At number 156 were the showrooms of Storr and Mortimer, later Hunt and Roskell, the royal goldsmiths. The Doré Gallery at number 35 sold 'choice products' of the French artist Gustave Doré. These were joined by Agnew's, the Grosvenor Gallery and the Fine Art Society. There were good bookshops, too: Hookham's, Ebers's (where the novelist Harrison Ainsworth worked for a time) and Brindley's, whose original triangular-shaped façade survived until 1931, ending its days as 'Ellis's, the Oldest Bookshop in London'.

But alongside the galleries and bookshops were workaday provisions merchants. One of the earliest Bond Street inhabitants was Austin the pieman, whose 'graceful effigies' are mentioned in Henry Carey's *Dissertation on Dumpling*. Nelson's Lady Hamilton, who lived in New Bond Street, bought her medicines and ointments from the chemist Savory and Moore a few doors away. The shop still has its original multi-paned Regency windows, as does Tessier's the jewellers opposite. Bond Street also contained drapers, milliners, cutlers, mercers, hosiers and butchers, many of them attracting attention to their businesses by gaudy hanging signs (the Turk's Head and Plume of Feathers, the Two Civet Cats and Olive Tree, the Flaming Sword) until a proclamation of 1762 required the removal of the signs, which were unsafe in high winds.

Tallis's *London Street Views* of 1840, with their charming front elevations of buildings, give a clear idea of the character of the street at the beginning of the decade in which Charles Asprey moved his business to Bond Street. At 49 New Bond Street we find 'Kennedy, Stationer and Dressing Case Maker'. At 47 were S. and T. Pratt, 'Importers of Antique Furniture, Armour, &c.'; at 48, Brewster, 'Peruke Maker and Perfumer to the Royal Family'; at 50, Chappell,

'Music Seller to Her Majesty', and at 51, Haines, Poulterer – a good cross-section of Bond Street commerce of the 1840s. The only one of these shops still in Bond Street is Chappell, to whose new silvery space-age façade a wit recently applied the first two lines of Daniel Defoe's *True-Born Englishman*:

> Wherever God erects a house of prayer,
> The Devil always builds a *Chappell* there.

The Move
to Number 166,
and Expansion

In 1847 the two Charles Aspreys broke with Kennedy and took the lease of 166 New Bond Street, the premises Asprey's now occupy, from Mrs Isabella Baldry, the widow of William C. Baldry who had run a mercer's business there for many years. (Subsequently they were able to buy the property and in 1861, by acquiring the rooms of Lord Byron's old haunt, the Alfred Club[3] at 22 Albemarle Street, they created a shop which stretched between Bond Street and Albemarle Street with entrances from each.)

Preparations were already well under way for the Great Exhibition of 1851, in which the finest manufacturers of the world were to be pitted against each other. Asprey's, who at that time advertised 'articles of exclusive design and high quality, whether for personal adornment or personal accompaniment and to endow with richness and beauty the tables and homes of people of refinement and discernment', decided to exhibit at the Crystal Palace. A dozen pieces of their finest workmanship were submitted and all were accepted for display. They carried off no gold or silver medals, but one of their dressing cases had an 'honourable mention' and is described in the official catalogue:

A ladies' dressing case in a specimen of rare wood, surmounted with a new design, descriptive of Neptune's attributes and a shield in the centre with the name of Anne in ciphers entwined, the whole executed in chased and gilt or-molu. Secret compartments for sovereigns, notes, jewellery, etc. The fittings form a complete set in cut glass with massive silver tops, each bearing the same name. A set of ivory brushes for the hair, for cloth and velvet and a pearl mounted

shoe-lift, poll and mouth-glass, all bearing the same name in relief. The cutlery and other instruments in white cornelian handles, mounted in gold with turquoise, etc. representing the 'Forget-me-not' and the linings in silk velvet.

An Adelaide Writing Desk, in Coromandel wood, with pierced, gilt, and engraved mounts, with china medallions, and fitted with every requisite for correspondence

DRESSING-CASE, INKSTAND, CASKETS, &C.—BY C. ASPREY.

The first is an elegant stand, of original design, in richly chased or molu, surmounted by an ink-glass in the form of an elaborately-executed vase, in or molu, with two figures blowing horns forming a pen-rest. The next article is an ebony casket, of superior workmanship and unique design, artistically arranged, with serpents upholding antique corals. The feet, handles, key, &c., are all elegantly and artistically wrought. The last is a jewel-casket or cabinet, also of original design, richly furnished, in or molu, set with malachite, arranged with drawers and folding doors, pierced and chased in relief, of superior workmanship.

(Original caption of 1851.)

A Travelling Bag, with Sterling Silver Fittings, richly engraved, and with silver locks, and containing everything necessary for the toilet, together with writing materials, and numerous other arrangements conducive to the comfort of travellers

In the 1850s, the old wooden dressing cases used by the gentry when they travelled about in their private coaches were being superseded by more portable and less cumbersome leather cases, suitable for travel on the fast-spreading railways. The Aspreys set out to capture this market. An early catalogue, undated but probably of the 1850s, illustrates gentlemen's dressing bags in Russia leather, containing two scent bottles, plated railway key (at that time passengers were still locked into the carriages for safety), jewel case, silver shaving brush and ivory-handled strop for cut-throat razors, at prices between £21 and £94.10s according to the number of fittings. But in the same catalogue dressing cases in coromandel wood, some with tortoiseshell and coral settings, were still being offered – at £400! In 1857 Charles Asprey II improved the design of his dressing cases by a new handle, patented in that year[4], which became standard for all high-quality dressing cases.

Pierced silver gallery double ink, Gadroon border and scroll feet

In 1859 Asprey's made the first of a series of adroit takeovers, absorbing the old-established firm of Edwards of 21 King Street, Holborn, which since 1817 had been the leading manufacturer of patent military mounted writing and dressing cases. In 1832 Thomas Jeyes Edwards had been appointed dressing-case maker to William IV, the Royal Family and the East India Company, but the highest recommendation from Asprey's point of view must have been the gold medal that Edwards won in the Great Exhibition for a gentleman's dressing case. 'This beautiful piece of workmanship, the catalogue rhapsodized, 'both tasteful and substantial, does infinite credit to the old-fashioned firm from whence it came. It consists of three distinct compartments, either of which can be raised to any convenient elevation and remain stationary, while required. The hinge is on a new principle, the invention (patent) of the exhibitor.'

Shortly after this success, Edwards had received the royal warrant as dressing-case, travelling-bag and writing-case maker to Queen Victoria. He was one of the first to turn from wood to leather and the exhibit which won him the gold medal was a transitional piece made of wood but covered with fine morocco leather. Asprey's benefited from Edwards's expertise, and from the skill of the trained workmen from King Street. In 1862, Asprey's also received a warrant from Queen Victoria, and Edwards stayed with the company until his retirement in 1872.

The effects of the influx of talent from Edwards's were seen at the International Exhibition of 1862, where Asprey's won a gold medal for excellence in dressing cases and took first place among the exhibitors in their class. Four pages of the official programme were devoted to their exhibits; some of these were new products, others were lent by customers such as Lady Lismore, Lady Harriet Ashley and Sir Alfred Tichbourne for whom Asprey's had been making dressing cases even before their Bond Street days. The programme suggested that 'a visit to Mr Asprey's establishment would repay anyone, where may be seen not only a splendid stock of exquisitely finished articles but, what is more, such articles in process of manufacture on the premises'.

It may have been through his associations with Kennedy and Edwards, both of King Street, Holborn, that Charles Asprey II took a keen interest in the Holborn Valley Improvement Scheme which

Lady's dressing case in Bengal wood, inlaid and mounted externally with brass, lined internally with velvet.

The fittings are of cut crystal glass with silver gilt tops; the large mirror can be adjusted to any angle, and on each side are two hand mirrors; beneath these are candle-branches so arranged as to fold in the lid. The fall front is fitted with a call-bell, mariner's compass, thermometer, whistle, magnifier, glove stretcher etc. etc.

There are ingeniously contrived drawers for jewels, bank-notes, gold coins etc. besides repositories for pen, ink and paper. (Original caption.)

Ladies' Dressing Bags—*continued.*

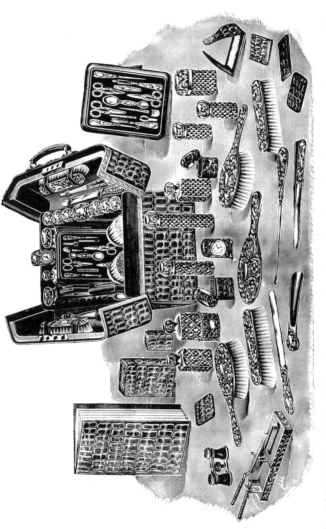

No. 25.—Size, 17½ inches long, 12 wide, 10¾ deep, in finest crocodile skin, and lined throughout the same, Asprey's patent double-action 4-link Bramah lock, and spring clips. Stands at each end to take out with the fittings. Containing:

Richly cut glass soap jar
" " tooth powder jar
" " pomade jar
" " tooth brush jar — with finest
" " nail brush jar — chased
" " powder jar — silver tops
2 " " scent bottles
" " and top
Chased silver 8-day clock
" " flask with finest chased silver cup

2 Finely chased silver hair brushes
2 " " clothes brushes
" " hand mirror
" " shoe horn
" " glove stretchers
" " paper knife
" " mounted button hook
" " inkstand
" " match box
" " curling tongs
" " penholder

A crocodile-skin case with glass lid, fitted with a set of chased silver instruments
Crocodile-skin blotting book
" " work case
" " pincushion
" " address book
" " plaister case
" " jewel case
" " covered curling lamp

£145 0 0

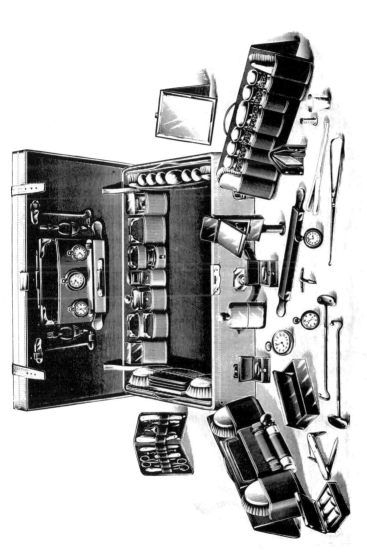

No. 49.—Size, 29½ inches long, 18½ wide, 7½ deep, in finest crocodile skin, lined red leather, with end stands to take out, 2 Asprey's patent double-action Bramah locks, containing :

Best rolled glass soap jar with rounded silver hinged top and finely pierced mount on the glass
   ,,   ,,   tooth-powder jar   ,,   ,,   and bayonet top
   ,,   ,,   tooth-brush jar   ,,   ,,
   ,,   ,,   shaving-brush jar   ,,   ,,
   ,,   ,,   pomade jar   ,,   ,,
   ,,   ,,   hair-wash bottle   ,,   ,,   and sprinkler,
Two ,,   ,,   scent bottles   ,,   ,,
Solid silver flask with bayonet-jointed top
Compass in silver case
2 silver-mounted horn cups
Best plated railway lantern
Corkscrew and railway key
2 best ivory extra thick hair brushes

Large morocco silver-mounted blotting book
  ,,   ,,   case of razors, scissors, &c.
  ,,   ,,   jewel case
  ,,   ,,   cigarette case
  ,,   ,,   card case
  ,,   ,,   looking glass
  ,,   ,,   inkstand and match box
  ,,   ,,   medicine case
  ,,   ,,   glass case
Best ivory extra thick paper knife
  ,,   ,,   -handled boot hooks
  ,,   ,,   strop
  ,,   ,,   tortoiseshell comb

Aneroid barometer in silver case
Silver large watch
Best ivory extra thick clothes brush
  ,,   ,,   ,,   hat brush
  ,,   ,,   ,,   hat rim brush
  ,,   ,,   ,,   glove stretchers

£125 0 0

resulted in the building of Holborn Viaduct. In 1863 the Corporation of London instituted a competition for architects, engineers and others to submit designs for 'raising Holborn Valley and making such alterations and improvements in and adjacent to Holborn Hill and Skinner Street, as would conduce to the convenience of the public, and to the accommodation of the Metropolitan traffic'. Advertisements were placed in newspapers and premiums of £250 and £150 were offered for the two designs most approved (though the Corporation cagily reserved the right not to use the winning design). Charles Asprey decided to enter. The judging committee had to consider 105 designs from 84 designers; these were illustrated by 206 drawings and 13 models and the bewildered committee resolved to call on the services of William Haywood, Surveyor to the Commissioners of Sewers, to assist them in the judging. Haywood was a competitor himself but agreed to withdraw his own designs and prepare a report on the others. The winners were Richard Bell (£250) and Thomas Charles Sorby (£150). The plans of six other designers received honourable mention but these did not include Charles Asprey's. The Viaduct was opened by Queen Victoria on 6 November 1869. The cost of the Viaduct and approaches, including the purchase of land, was £2,552,406; Haywood's original estimate was £226,988.[5]

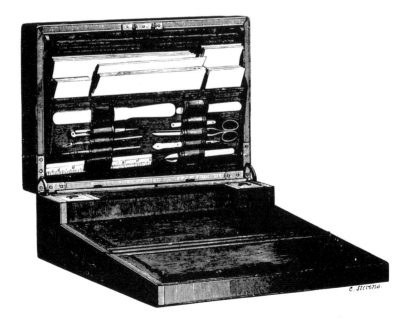

Asprey's continued to consolidate their position in the late nineteenth century by shrewd takeovers. In 1888 they acquired W. Leuchars, a firm which had been in Piccadilly since 1794, first as a perruquier and then, as wigs went out of fashion, as a dressing-case maker. They were suppliers of dressing cases to William IV's consort, Queen Adelaide. Leuchars also became accomplished goldsmiths and silversmiths: Mr Leuchars 'would never demean himself by advertising his wares'. By taking over Leuchars, Asprey's removed one of their main rivals. In 1884, Leuchars themselves had absorbed the firm of Louis Dee, founded by Thomas William Dee about 1830. Dee's had been wholesale working jewellers, mounting Victorian enamels, wood and other materials in gold and silver.[6] It seems that Asprey's had a more direct connection with Dee's than the mere takeover of Leuchars as George Dewey, who worked at Asprey's all his life until his retirement in 1948, recalled in a letter of 1953:

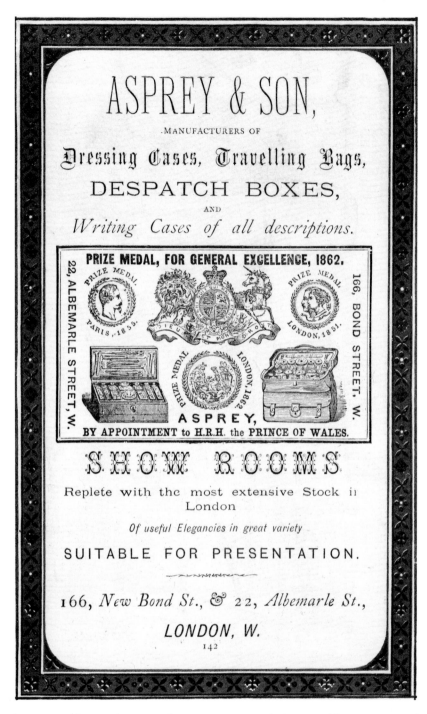

An advertisement, for an unknown catalogue or magazine, which appeared between 1862 and 1870

Messrs Asprey acquired their Factory from a famous London silversmith, Mr Louis Dee of Sherwood St. W, and added to it a manufactory of finest leather goods. This Factory was moved to Heddon St., then to Bird St., then to Euston Road, and finally to the upper floors of 165–8 Bond Street and 22 Albermarle St., where it now carries on the production of both leather goods and gold and silversmiths' work...

Dewey also remembered that when Asprey's acquired Leuchars' Piccadilly premises, Leuchars' Paris branch was taken over by Mr Geoffroy of 2, rue de la Paix, formerly manager at Leuchars. Geoffroy continued to buy many of Asprey's products and was their Paris agent until 1902. In that year, Dewey recalled:

Messrs Charles and George Asprey sold the lease of Nos 38 and 39 Piccadilly (Leuchars) to Messrs Thomas Cook and Son, the well known travel and theatre agents, who occupied the premises as their West End offices. The stock of dressing bags and cases and silver goods was transferred to Asprey's Bond Street premises. Nearly all the Piccadilly staff were engaged for work at Bond St. Mr A.W. Hilling became a partner in the firm of Asprey. About this time, Messrs Asprey acquired the lease of No. 15a Grafton Street from Messrs Last, leather trunk makers. The dividing walls of the shop were removed and new windows fitted, with a side door in Grafton Street. The first floor was let to the late Sir Henry Irving.

Irving was the last great private resident of Bond Street, which in the past had housed Laurence Sterne, Boswell, Sir Thomas Lawrence and Lord Nelson. His quarters were above Asprey's, and the front door may still be seen at 15a Grafton Street. The house was described in the *Strand Magazine*:

The staircase of the house is replete with grand bronzes. One of Don Quixote is just opposite the dining-room door. Here, too, are many views of Venice and a number of sketches by Seymour Lucas. The dining room overlooks Bond Street. It is a distinctly comfortable room. A bust of Kemble is over the bookcase, with another of Dante. The exquisite Spanish ware is to be envied. On one side of the mantelpiece is an interesting reminiscence of Mrs Siddons – a picture of 'The Shoulder of Mutton Inn', Brecon, South Wales, where she was born...

Today, a plaque on the house records that Irving lived there from 1872 to 1899. Naturally, he was a frequent customer of Asprey's, his landlords.

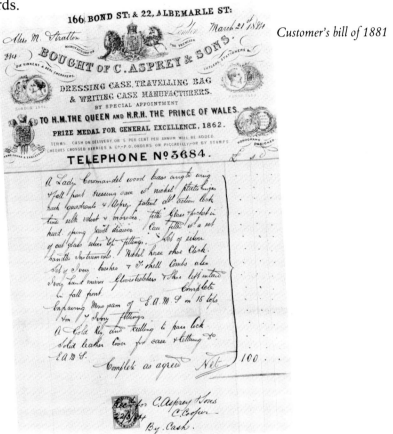

Customer's bill of 1881

In 1904 Asprey's further extended their premises by acquiring 167 New Bond Street from Keith Prowse, giving them 159 New Bond Street in exchange. In the early twentieth century, they bought out two of their New Bond Street neighbours: in 1906 they acquired the business of Houghton and Gunn, who since 1822 had been high-class leather goods manufacturers and stationers at number 161; and in 1911 they took over William Payne and Company, who had been watchmakers at number 163 since 1838. The craftsmen of these firms joined the Asprey work force.

The Reign of
Edward VII

By the beginning of the century, Asprey's were the acknowledged leaders in their field. There were other excellent dressing-case makers in the West End – Mappin and Webb, Fisher of the Strand, John Pound of Leadenhall Street, Drew and Sons of Piccadilly Circus, Alexander Clark of Oxford Street and Fenchurch Street, J.W. Benson of Ludgate Hill and the Goldsmiths' and Silversmiths' Company of Regent Street. But Asprey's were rather more than *primus inter pares*; in 1889 they had gained a further royal warrant as suppliers to the Prince of Wales, who succeeded to the throne as King Edward VII on the death of Queen Victoria in 1901. Edward VII was so delighted with the monogram Asprey's designed for the cigarette case they made him, that he suggested to Austen Chamberlain, Postmaster-General in Balfour's Cabinet, that the device (E_R) should be used on pillar-boxes. But kings' whims no longer had quite the same force as in Henry VIII's reign, and the idea was rejected.

Mr Percy Hubbard, who came to Asprey's in the middle of Edward's reign, had vivid memories of those days:

> Bond Street presented a very different appearance then. All traffic was horse-drawn. There was no omnibus or taxi. The customers arrived in carriages – broughams, phaetons and dog-carts, and invariably had their footmen. During one day, I would see customers in here in three different modes of dress: morning, afternoon and evening – we kept open until half-past six in those days. Some customers would call in on their way to a party to buy gifts. Of course all the men wore silk hats, which they doffed as they came in the door – the same door that you see today. At that time, when Guards officers

were men of means, it was a common sight to see them in the late hours of the morning in their long black frock coats, escorting actresses from the Gaiety, Daly's and other theatres.

The year was divided into two seasons: just before Easter until Cowes, and then October to Christmas. The other times were quiet times. Among my early tasks was to take a selection of goods round to Lord Rosebery in Berkeley Square, so he could choose presents for his grandchildren.

At that time the firm was run by Charles and George Asprey. 'Charles was the elder brother, very stern, very fair; but his brother George, who was business manager and later took over as chairman, was very popular, he had a wonderful way.' Hubbard had to work hard: 'Everyone who came in at that time was thoroughly trained by people who knew their business from A to Z. I started in the stockroom, under the stockroom manager Cooper. My job was to enter goods in stock and put tickets on them.' But there were moments of glamour to relieve the routine: 'The Empress Eugénie used to come in quite a lot because she had a place down in Farnborough: she died there and has a marvellous tomb there. She was very charming. Of course I did not wait upon her, but I remember it so well. She was getting on in age then, but she was perfectly attired, very soberly.' Mr Hubbard also had affectionate memories of Princess Ena of Battenburg: 'When she married, they lived on the Isle of Wight. The people of the Isle of Wight gave her for her wedding a crocodile dressing case which we made. A few years ago she was in here. She greeted me, and I said "How's the dressing case?" "Oh," she said, "unfortunately the dressing case is no more; but I still use the fittings."' By the time Mr Hubbard joined Asprey's, leather dressing cases had almost entirely superseded wooden ones, 'but we still had a few wooden ones in stock'. Trunks for the royal family were made in black leather instead of the normal brown.

Mr Hubbard had a clear memory of Edward VII's funeral: 'Practically all the ruling heads of Europe were there, and many of them came to Asprey's: you might see three or four in the shop at one time. Of course, I was still very much a junior.' For George V's Coronation, Bond Street was decorated with triumphal festoons designed by Sir Frank Brangwyn, and Asprey's were among the subscribers who paid for these. The royal patronage of Asprey's

continued in the new reign: 'When the late Queen Mary came in, Mr George Asprey would wait upon her. She always came in before Christmas to get her presents.' Just before the First World War, some suffragettes threw bricks through Asprey's plate glass windows to draw attention to their cause. George Dewey, who was present, recorded with satisfaction, 'The offenders were promptly arrested and punished.' In 1912, Asprey's slide-action cigarette case was introduced; it was said that every smart young officer in the Great War had to own an Asprey cigarette case and a Dunhill pipe.

ASPREY & CO.,

165-166, NEW BOND STREET, LONDON, W.

COMMUNICATING WITH 22, ALBEMARLE STREET

ALL GOODS SOLD FOR CASH AT ACTUAL MAKERS' PRICES.

ASPREY'S WORKS ARE:

19-21, HEDDON STREET, LONDON, W.

IN presenting their 1905 List of Articles suitable for Presents, Messrs. ASPREY desire to call attention to the very moderate prices quoted. This is only possible by reason of their newly adopted system of trading for cash only, which has caused instant and remarkable expansion in their business.

ASPREY & CO.

HAVE

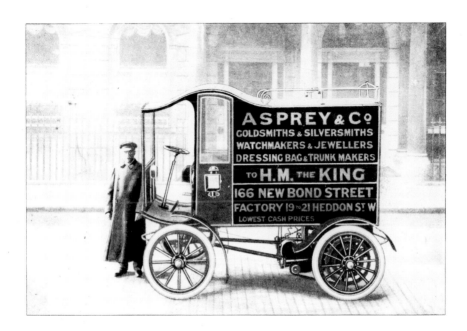

UNIQUE FACILITIES FOR EXPRESS DELIVERY.

Toast Racks, etc.

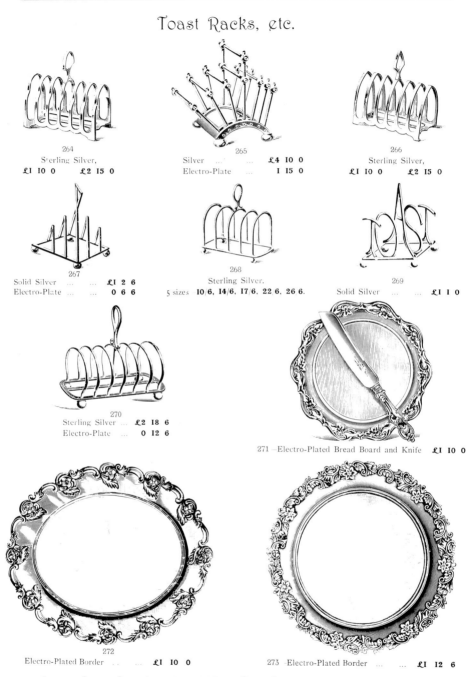

264
Sterling Silver,
£1 10 0   £2 15 0

265
Silver   ...   £4 10 0
Electro-Plate   ...   1 15 0

266
Sterling Silver,
£1 10 0   £2 15 0

267
Solid Silver £1 2 6
Electro-Plate 0 6 6

268
Sterling Silver.
5 sizes   10/6, 14/6, 17/6, 22 6, 26 6.

269
Solid Silver £1 1 0

270
Sterling Silver ...   £2 18 6
Electro-Plate   ...   0 12 6

271 —Electro-Plated Bread Board and Knife   £1 10 0

272
Electro-Plated Border £1 10 0

273 —Electro-Plated Border £1 12 6

A selection of pages from Asprey's 1905 List of Articles

Dessert Knives and Forks.

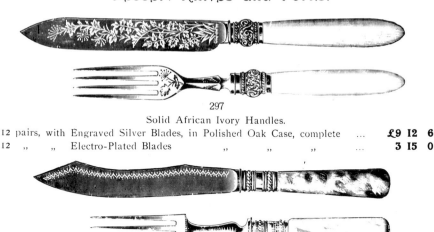

297

Solid African Ivory Handles.

12 pairs, with Engraved Silver Blades, in Polished Oak Case, complete ...	£9 12	6
12 ,, ,, Electro-Plated Blades ,, ,, ,, ...	3 15	0

298

Finest Pearl Handles.

12 pairs, with Silver Blades, in Polished Oak Case, complete	£8 17	6
12 ,, ,, Electro-Plated Blades ,, ,, ,, ...	3 10	0

299

Solid African Ivory Handles.

12 pairs, with Silver Blades, in Polished Oak Case, complete	£8 12	6
12 ,, ,, Electro-plated Blades ,, ,, ,, ...	3 7	6

300

Thread Pattern.

12 pairs, all Solid Silver, in Polished Oak Case, complete	£11 15	0
12 ,, in Finest Electro-Plate ,, ,, ,, ...	3 10	0

Prices of other Patterns on application. Ask for quotation before deciding elsewhere.

Cut-Glass Champagne Jugs.—Mounted either with Silver or finest Electro-Plate.

WITH A FULL SIZED ICE CHAMBER FITTED TO EACH.

93

To take	Electro-Plate.	Silver.
1 bottle	**£3 2 6**	**£6 10 0**
Magnum	**3 15 0**	**7 17 6**

94

A beautifully Hand-made and Chased Silver Water Jug, of handsome outline and ornament.

£15 10 0

95

To take	Electro-Plate.	Silver.
1 bottle	**£3 15 0**	**£7 10 0**
Magnum	**4 10 0**	**8 10 0**

96

To take	Electro-Plate.	Silver.
1 bottle	**£3 5 0**	**£7 0 0**
Magnum	**3 18 6**	**8 10 0**

97

To take	Electro-Plate.	Silver.
1 bottle	**£3 7 6**	**£6 17 6**
Magnum	**3 17 6**	**8 0 0**

98

To take	Electro-Plate.	Silver.
1 bottle	**£3 15 0**	**£8 7 6**
Magnum	**4 15 0**	**9 10 0**

The handles of these Jugs being made in Silver or Electro-Plate are much stronger than if made of glass, as is usually the case.

Solid Silver and Finest Electro-Plated Lamps, etc.

Corinthian Design,
Solid Silver,
Cut Glass, and
Silk Shade,
Complete, £21 0 0

Finest Electro-Plate,
Complete,
£8 10 0

519

518

520

Shell Design.

Solid Silver, 3-light, £23 15 0 per pair.
„ 5-light, 33 0 0 „

Corinthian Design.

Solid Silver, 3-light, £26 15 0 per pair.
„ 5-light, 36 15 0 „

Prices in best Electro-Plate on application.

The First World War

Business was 'very badly affected' by the war, Dewey recalls, 'but a department supplying military camp equipment was formed and was of great use to officers of the Services. Also a caravan-marquee was sent to Salisbury Plain Camp, for the sale of equipment'. A letter from a satisfied client is preserved in Asprey's archives:

Flanders, December 4, 1915

Asprey's,
Bond Street, London.

Gentlemen,

Please accept my thanks for the Pig hide Sam Browne you made me. After being assured by several of the reputed 'live' firms who made leather goods their special effort that being Englishmen they couldn't make a pig hide belt because they had never heard of one and also that there were no pig hides to be had in London, it was quite refreshing to find someone who was willing to get out of the rut and answer an unusual demand by an unusual effort. If you had taken 24 days instead of 24 hours to make my belt I would not have been surprised: as it is, I am thrilled to death. The Colt holster & clip case are both A.1.

Wishing you every success,

Yours truly,
A.D.Cockrill (Lt.)
5th Canadians.

GERMAN SHELL FUSE,
MOUNTED AS A
PENWIPER

GERMAN BULLET
UNDER GLASS
PAPERWEIGHT

GERMAN
RIFLE BULLETS
AS PENCILS AND
LETTER-OPENER

TOP LIFTS
OFF FROM
HERE FOR
CIGAR BOX

INK STAND

INCENDIARY BOMB CONVERTED INTO
CIGAR BOX AND LIGHTER

POUNDER SHELL CASE AS A GONG

GERMAN SHELL FUSES AS PAPERWEIGHTS

In the early days of the war, Kenneth Asprey obtained a commission in the Scots Guards and served during the terrible battles on the Somme. Mr Philip Asprey also obtained a commission in the Buffs and served in Flanders and the Near East, being awarded the M.C. and the Croix de Guerre. His brother, Captain Maurice Asprey, was killed in action.

Some conventional luxury-goods business continued during the First World War in an auxiliary factory over the Bruton Mews Garage, which Asprey's had acquired ('Telephone Mayfair 4282–A Garage that is Conveniently Placed in the Midst of the Best Shops, Theatres & Hotels'). Mr G.W. Knapp wrote to Mr Eric Asprey in 1976:

When the time arrived for me to start at Asprey's, I decided I would prefer to make things instead of selling, so in 1916 I started work at Factory 2 which was over the garage in Bruton Mews. This was a small, dusty workshop with the fumes from the cars below, but some of the most beautiful work was turned out, such as fitted motor bags, and dressing cases with cut glass fittings, gold-topped bottles with diamond monograms, etc., selling in those days up to £1,000.

I used to call round to Bond Street on queries to Mr Bowring, Mr Hayes, Mr Knapp, Mr Grew, etc., all fine men and well experienced in the finest of work. Mr Betlem I remember well–what a great artist!

Of the staff here mentioned, 'Mr Knapp' was G.W. Knapp's own father, who had begun work at Asprey's in 1894. Mr Grew was the senior assistant who 'waited upon' the Prince of Wales (later Edward VIII): the photograph below shows Grew with the Prince in the boathouse. And 'Mr Betlem' deserves special mention, as one of the most distinguished artists who ever worked for Asprey's.

Mr Grew with the Duke of Windsor in the upper part of Asprey's known as 'the boathouse'

Jacobus Betlem

Jacobus Betlem (1883-1950) was the second son of Pieter Betlem of Zaandijk, Holland[7]. He had three brothers and three sisters. After a rudimentary schooling he was apprenticed to his father at the age of twelve as a painter and decorator. Zaandijk was a fairly prosperous town – an inland port handling a lot of timber. Most of the houses in the area were built of wood and their upkeep was his father's main business. Betlem's earliest days were spent painting the sails and upper parts of the windmills that abounded in the surrounding country, but he also sketched in oils and water-colour and was ambitious to work in a higher sphere of art than painting windmill sails. Attracted by the growing socialist movement, he was active in local political parties. Betlem obtained work with a high-class decorator who encouraged him to go abroad and extend his experience – partly, perhaps, because his fervent socialism was becoming an embarrassment. But Betlem was shocked out of his socialism by the discovery that one of the party officials had spirited away the party funds, a considerable sum. 'From that time on,' his son records, 'he gave up all brands of politics and to my knowledge had the strongest objection to voting at any election. This was his only aberration from – what all who knew him remember – his love and confidence in his fellow men.'

In 1906 Betlem went to Amsterdam Central Station and wondered whether he should book a ticket to Rome, London or New York, all then in the *avant-garde* of interior design and furnishing. London won because a friend from his home town lived there. Betlem knew no English but managed to find lodgings in Chelsea, and took with him round the streets a sketch-book in which his friend had written: 'The bearer of this letter is J. Betlem, a skilled Dutch painter. He requires work and would be pleased if you would write a reply if he could work for you and where and what time he is to report.' This he took to any site where work was in progress, and obtained freelance work for some years. He also enrolled at the Regent Street Polytechnic, where he was asked what he could do. But his English was so bad that as the teacher took him to each class he said 'Too easy!' meaning just the opposite; so he finished in the hardest class of all, drawing the human model from life. He went on to win more medals for his work than any previous student.

Betlem was doing some piece-work for Asprey's in 1910, and the foreman was asked whether there was anyone in his team who could draw. 'The Dutchman is quite good,' he said, and Betlem was offered the job. The result was a further commission and eventually a permanent post. His son wrote after his death: 'My father's skills were such that he was able very professionally to decorate and design interiors and exteriors of houses and buildings, sketch, paint and draw in all sorts of mediums. He was also an expert miniaturist and excelled in lettering, illuminating and gilding. He had a number of oil paintings accepted and hung in the Royal Academy.' The biggest task Asprey's ever entrusted to him was the interior decoration of Captain Wolf Barnato's house at Gatwick in 1934. 'Here,' his son recalled, 'he was able to demonstrate his skills to the full, even to showing painters how to mix the colours he required for the rooms. His skill at wood graining was great, and many wondered where wood began and metal ended. His tragedy was in seeing this great work destroyed before his eyes in a disastrous fire just prior to completion in 1934.'[8] Betlem's greatest ambition – to win a major British award for jewellery – was thwarted by the very excellence of the standards Asprey's demanded, since he found himself unable to work down to the cost criteria stipulated in the competition. As his son relates, 'His long experience at Asprey's had ingrained the habit that the object was the prime thing and not the cost. Opulence was his master.'

THE LUXURIOUS

1920s

Charles Asprey died in 1916 and the well-loved 'Mr George' in 1918, when Lionel Asprey became chairman of the company which had been formed in 1909.[9] Philip Asprey joined the firm in 1919, becoming manager of the factory on his father's death in 1921. Mr Eric Asprey joined in 1924. The biggest-spending clients of Asprey's in the 1920s were Americans and Indian maharajahs. The American millionaires included J. Pierpont Morgan who ordered all his dressing cases from the firm. In 1927 Saks of Fifth Avenue became Asprey's American agent. The maharajahs included the Maharajahs of Patiala and Cooch Behar, the Gaekwar of Baroda and the Sultan of Lahore. They get two mentions in Sir John Betjeman's autobiographical poem *Summoned by Bells*. Describing his father's furniture factory in Pentonville Road, he writes:

> When you rang
> The front-door bell a watchful packer pulled
> A polished lever twenty yards away,
> And this released the catch into a world
> Of shining showrooms full of secret drawers
> And Maharajahs' dressing-cases.

John Betjeman was an only son, and his father hoped he would join the family firm – the fourth generation to do so. But already the boy had set his heart on being a poet; he confesses that for him there was no beauty in the

> polished wood and stone
> Tortured by Father's craftsmen into shapes
> To shine in Asprey's showrooms under glass,
> A Maharajah's eyeful.

Asprey's workshop before the Second World War

This was, of course, a somewhat jaundiced view. It is generally agreed today that the workmanship of G. Betjemann and Sons had no equal in the England of its period. All timber used was left outside the Pentonville Road factory for two years to weather, and was then brought in under a gantry to weather again, so that it would be perfectly seasoned. Upstairs in the factory were stocks of the best veneers that could be found: walnut, satinwood, Thuyawood, macassar and ebony. Recently Asprey's bought back from a customer an ivory-angled finely figured Thuyawood games cabinet made by Betjemann's for Asprey in about 1930, complete with *chemin-de-fer* shoe, twelve packs of playing-cards, leather draughts board, dominoes, dice, draughts, poker chips and baccarat cloth. It sold originally for £99.10s. Betjemann's also made for Asprey boxes of onyx, lapis lazuli and malachite, cigar boxes, cigarette boxes of fine woodwork and ashtrays. Asprey's still sell an onyx cigarette box with the patent Betjemann hinge, which has a spring in its knuckle that causes the lid to shut gently, not with a snap, so that the onyx will not crack.

The biggest maharajah commission came in 1930, during the Round Table Conference on India held in London, when the Indian princes stayed in London hotels. Mr F.P. Threadgill, a former employee of Betjemann and Sons, recalls: 'The Maharajah of Patiala was in the Haymarket Hotel. Through Asprey's, we were given the commission to make huge teak trunks, one for each of his five wives. Each trunk was fitted with solid silver washing and bathing utensils – bowls, wash-basins, hand-basins, soap boxes, soap dishes, tooth-brush holders. The bottles for pouring hot water had spouts with tigers' heads. We had to work overtime on it, it was a terrific job.' Mr William Hammond, another employee of Ernest Betjemann at the time, more ribaldly recalled that the toilet sets contained 'goes-unders – you know, goesunder the bed – in eighth-inch silver.' He added:

> The Union at that time allowed no bonuses of any kind. But when that job was completed, Mr Ernest Betjemann asked us all to leave a registered envelope at the office, and we all received a cheque according to our standing in the factory, from ten bob for the shop-boy upwards; I got £5. I made the teakwork for the outside and cut all the openings for the

various things to lie in and Bill Jones – probably the best cabinet-maker at Betjemann's – assembled the cases, and George Baker lined them with blue velvet.

Betjemann's were also employed by Asprey's on another sumptuous commission – to refurnish the large house of Captain Wolf Barnato, the racing driver, at Gatwick. The house included a big music room, Mr Hammond recalls, 'where the whole wall went up, revealing a bar lined with coloured mirrors'. Unfortunately, there was a fault in the electrical wiring and, as already mentioned, the house was burnt out in 1934, just before the work was completed.

Ernest Betjemann was a keen antique collector, and it was his interest in eighteenth-century antiques that gave him the idea of reviving shagreen work, which was made not from sharkskin as is commonly believed but from Japanese stingray skin. The shagreen skins were dyed green, pink or blue, and through Asprey's the fashion became the rage in London for a while. Betjemann was also one of the first manufacturers to realize that some concession must be made to the new style, now known as 'Art Deco' but then called 'moderne' or 'Jazz modern', introduced by the Paris Exposition des Arts Décoratifs in 1925. Asprey's catalogues of the 1920s and 1930s are, for today's collectors of Art Deco, mouthwatering anthologies. This was the age of cocktails, and Ernest Betjemann's foreman, Horace Andrew, designed a particularly Art Deco cocktail cabinet for sale at Asprey's – the 'elevette' in which the bottles rose to the top when one pressed a handle; it worked on the principle of an inverted bicycle pump.

Philip Asprey and Ernest Betjemann became great friends. Obviously it was politic for Betjemann to get on well with a member of the family who sold so many of Betjemann and Sons' goods; but from the moment of their first meeting in 1919, when Philip Asprey was still 'working his way up from the bottom' under the exacting surveillance of Dewey (by then the stockroom keeper at Asprey's) the two took to each other. They were temperamentally alike – diligent and scrupulous in business, and happiest when out in the open with gun, rod or golf club. Asprey used to drive Betjemann in his open Singer sports car down to Betjemann's fishing club on a tributary of the Kennet beyond Reading, to fish for trout. He and his brother Eric stayed at the Rock Hotel, Cornwall, to join Betjemann

The most original and practical Christmas Gift..

ASPREY'S

Joy-Bell

COCKTAIL SHAKER

Capacity 1½ pints. Ample room for ice.

FINEST SILVER PLATED

£2.17.6

SOLID SILVER
£11.10.0

A really original and attractive Cocktail Set. You swing the bell to shake the cocktail and your guests ring for a refill by tinkling their joy-bell glasses . . .

THE SHAKER AND SIX GLASSES MAKE A PERFECT GIFT.

Novel joy-bell glasses with clappers in 6 different colours 8/6 EACH.

Asprey

BOND STREET, LONDON, W.1
C.F.H.

*The age of cocktails –
the Joy-Bell cocktail shaker was a
beautiful example of Asprey's Art-Deco range*

in golf on the St Enodoc course. After one of these holidays, Eric Asprey gave John Betjeman a lift back to London in his snub-nosed Bentley. He remembers John, then still a schoolboy, leaning over the dashboard and shouting, 'Faster! Faster!'

It was Ernest Betjemann who introduced Philip Asprey to shooting:

> He said, 'Come up to shoot at the week-end.' I said: 'I haven't even got a gun.' So he said: 'Go on, buy one.' So I went down to Vaughan in the Strand and bought a gun: £20 it cost, best gun I ever had. I used to drive him up on Thursday nights to Mundford, the headquarters of the shoot. We took over the King's Arms, a tiny little pub run by a Mr and Mrs Gaskin. All feather beds, and magnificent food. I later took a small shoot of three hundred acres adjoining his, and borrowed his keeper, Jones, a local man, to look after it. Ernest Betjemann was a crack shot. But because he was stone deaf, and couldn't tell whether the birds were up or have any idea where they were coming from, he had Jones walk behind him to tap him on the shoulder and point. We used to bring back a tremendous amount of birds – partridge, pheasant or duck – and these would be distributed among the staff of Asprey's and Betjemann's.

Eric Asprey also came up sometimes, and more rarely John Betjeman would make up the party, a reluctant and erratic shot. After Ernest Betjemann's death in 1934, Philip Asprey became the main adviser to his widow on her business affairs, including the winding up of Betjemann and Sons just after the Second World War.

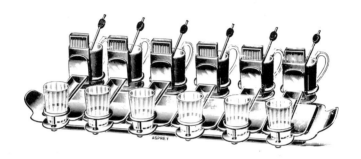

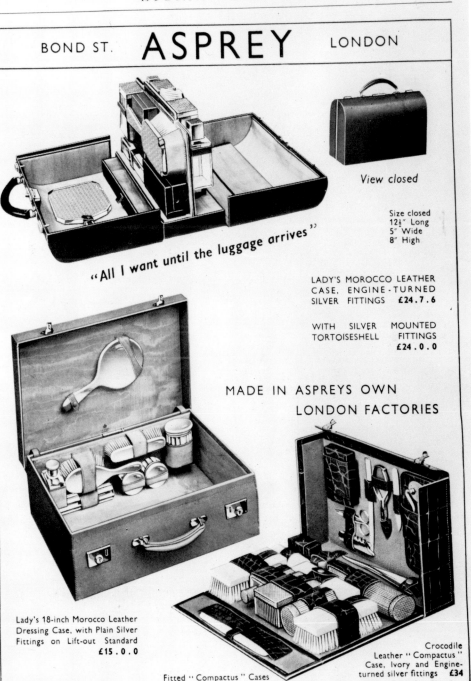

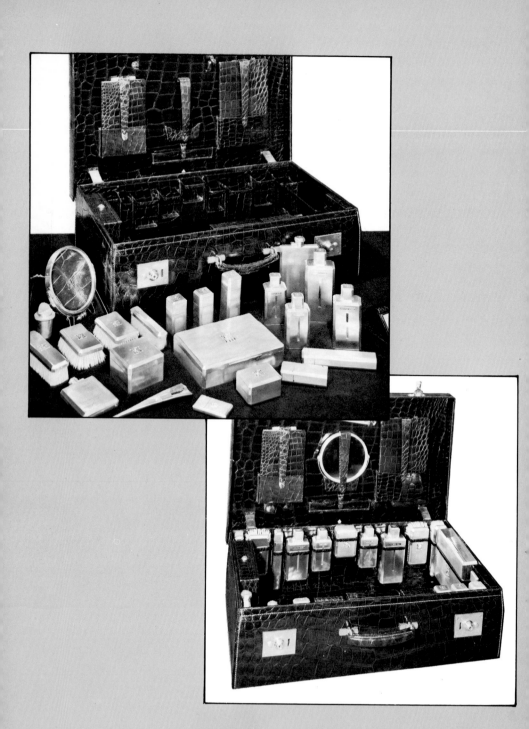

Golden crocodile 22-inch fitted case, with removable tray containing lady's silver dressing-table set,
comprising: hand mirror, hair brush, hat and cloth brushes, comb, 2 bottles, 2 cream jars, powder bowl,
soap dish, 2 small pots

Pigskin 22-inch fitted case, with removable tray containing gentleman's dressing-table set comprising 2 silver oblong military hair brushes and cloth brush, comb, 4 bottles, soap jar, manicure set, stud boxes, also empty compartments for other toiletries

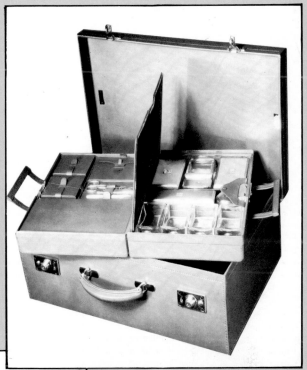

Cedar crocodile 24-inch fitted case with silver fittings, comprising set of 4 military brushes, comb, 4 bottles, 2 spirit flasks, shaving mirror, alarm clock, and various other containers

77

PATENT EJECTOR, CIGARETTE OR CIGAR TUBES.

FINEST BLOCK AMBER. 18-ct. Gold Mounts.

A very ingenious device which prevents burning the holder and easily ejects the end of cigarette or cigar.

CIGARETTE TUBES.

Size	2 in.	2½ in.	2¾ in.	2⅞ in.	3⅛ in.	3⅝ in.
Price	16/6	20/6	21/6	23/6	25/6	27/6

CIGAR TUBES.

Size	2⅜ in.	2⅝ in.	2¾ in.	2¼ in.	3½ in.	3¾ in.
Price	21/6	28/6	33/6	36/6	41/-	44/-

ASPREY'S
AUTOMATIC PENCIL SHARPENER.
THE ONLY PERFECT SHARPENER MADE.

	£ s. d.
Black metal	0 10 6
„ with oak or mahogany base ...	0 12 6
Electro-plate „ „ „ „ „ ...	1 1 0
Silver, with oak base	2 15 0
Silver, with silver base	3 15 0
Silver, with ivory base and handle	4 10 0

THE NEW ENAMELLED CIGARETTE TUBES.

All cut from the finest block amber, with beautifully enamelled mount, as illustrated.

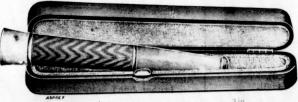

Also stocked with centre space for hygienic wad.

	3 in.	3½ in.	4½ in.
In various colours, each in red russia leather case	14/6	17/6	35/-

---

165, 166, and 167, NEW BOND STREET, and 22, ALBEMARLE STREET, W

SOLID SILVER

MOTOR FLOWER HOLDERS.

8 in. high, with Plated Ring Fixture,

£1 8s. 6d. complete.

THE "PRISCILLA" HAT-PIN STAND.

Height, 6 inches.

Sterling Silver, Pincushion Centre, 9/6.

AUTOMATIC CIGARETTE DELIVERER,

WITH MATCH BOX AT TOP.

Delivers one cigarette at a time.

Best Electro-plate, £1 15s.

Size, 7¼ by 3½ in.

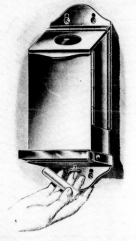

CINDERELLA PINCUSHION.

Beautifully made in finest Crushed Morocco and fitted — with Velvet Cushion. —

2/9 each.

ASPREY'S OWN LONDON MAKE.

ASPREY'S FRAMES

Are of full weight and strength, greatly differing from the poor quality frames sold elsewhere, which are very thin die-struck fronts, only deriving support from the backs to which they are fastened.

SOLID SILVER PHOTO FRAMES.

Cabinet Size, 6 × 4½ in.	...	15/6
Narrow ,, 6½ × 3½ in.	...	20/-
Imperial ,, 9½ × 7½ in.	...	35/-
Panel ,, 12⅞ × 8½ in.	...	75/-

165, 166, and 167, NEW BOND STREET, and 22, ALBEMARLE STREET, W.

SOLID SILVER MATCH BOXES.

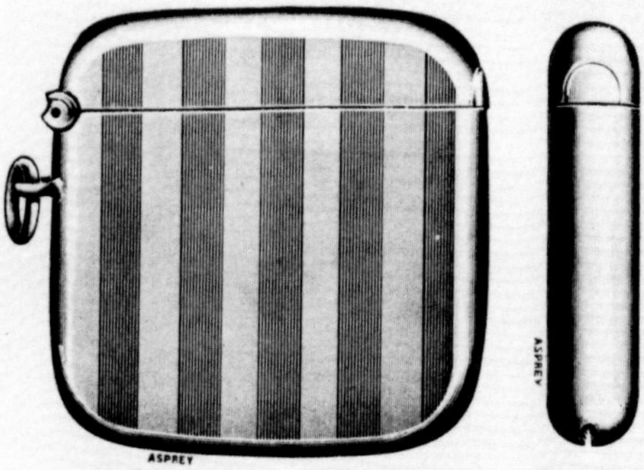
ASPREY
ASPREY

End View.

Size 1½ × 1½ inches	...	£0 8 6
,, 1¾ × 1¾ ,,	...	0 11 0
,, 2 × 2 ,,	...	0 13 6
,, 2¼ × 2¼ ,,	...	0 15 6

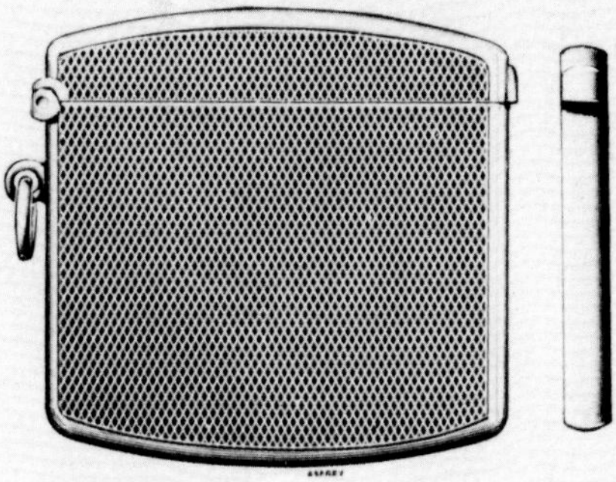

End View

Size 1¾ × 1⅞ inches	...	£0 13 6
,, 2⅛ × 2 ,,	...	0 15 6

ALL THESE PATTERNS CAN BE HAD IN 9-CT. OR 18-CT. GOLD.
PRICES WILL BE SENT ON APPLICATION.

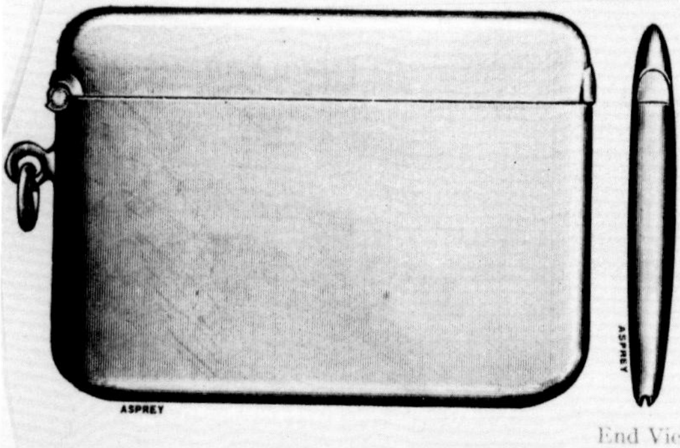
ASPREY
ASPREY

End View.

Size 1½ × 2 inches	...	£0 8 6
,, 2¼ × 1⅞ ,,	...	0 10 6
,, 2⅝ × 1⅞ ,,	...	0 12 6

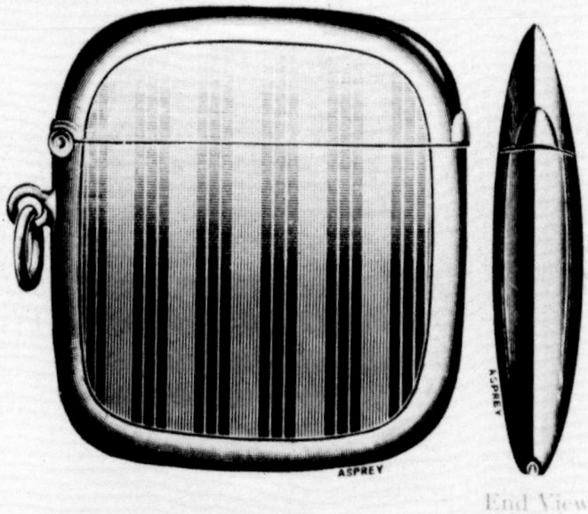
ASPREY
ASPREY

End View.

Size 1½ × 1½ inches	...	£0 7 0
,, 1⅞ × 1¾ ,,	...	0 10 6
,, 2 × 1⅞ ,,	...	0 12 6
,, 2⅜ × 2¼ ,,	...	0 15 0

ASPREY & CO., LTD.

CIGAR AND CIGARETTE LIGHTERS.

TORCH LIGHTERS.

Actual Sizes.

PRICES—LARGE SIZE.

Silver, plain ...	£0	6	6
Silver, engine-turned	0	7	6
9-ct. Gold, plain ...	2	0	0
9-ct. Gold, engine-turned ...	2	2	6
18-ct. Gold, plain...	4	5	0
18-ct. Gold, engine-turned ...	4	8	6

PRICES—SMALL SIZE.

Silver, plain ...	£0	5	6
Silver, engine-turned	0	6	6
9-ct. Gold, plain ...	1	15	0
9-ct. Gold, engine-turned ...	1	17	6
18-ct. Gold, plain...	3	12	6
18-ct. Gold, engine-turned ...	3	15	0

These lighters are filled with benzine and the torch remains always moist. The torch is withdrawn and struck on the patent metal edge to obtain a flame.

IMPERATOR LIGHTERS.

Actual Size.

NEW TABLE CIGAR AND CIGARETTE LIGHTERS.

WELL MADE IN DULL GILT METAL OF NEAT APPEARANCE, IN TWO SIZES.

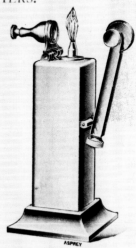

Sizes: 4¼ inches ...	£0	8	6
5½ ,, ...	0	10	6

These Lighters are unscrewed at the base for filling with benzine. Open the cap or extinguisher backwards as illustrated, press the right hand lever towards the lighter and turn the small wheel quickly. The sparks will then ignite the wick.

Silver, plain...	£0	5	6
Silver, engine-turned ...	0	6	6
9-ct. Gold, plain	1	15	0
9-ct. Gold, engine-turned ...	1	17	6
18-ct. Gold, plain	4	5	0
18-ct. Gold, engine-turned	4	7	6

THIS DAINTY TENNIS FROCK is of ivory washing silk. The contrasting bands of amber are inlet with hem-stitching. It can be copied in several attractive shades.

4½ guineas

A smart molyneux belt finishes this charming hat of white stitched linen, which is piped with contrasting bands of leather. It is designed as a complement to the frock.

Asprey
Bond St.
London

An Original Model by Lucien Lelong in Vanille Satin Beauté.

Original Model Picture Frock in Powder Blue Poulte-de-Soie and Silver Lace.

Original Champcomunal Model Evening Gown in Heavy Black Crêpe Marocain with crystal buckles

BOND STREET Asprey LONDON

Asprey
Bond St.
London

In this charming black felt model a new note is achieved by the introduction of tuscan straw in the brim. 6 gns.

Very becoming is this model in black satin with an under-lining of gold kid. 6½ gns.

a short period Asprey's offered a selection of fashion garments

Bond St Asprey London

THE NOVELTY OF TO-DAY
AND NEED OF THE MOMENT.
ALWAYS SOMETHING NEW AT ASPREY'S.

DISC
MATCH
HOLDERS

DISC
MATCH
HOLDERS

Silver, Engine-turned - 2.15.0
" Plain - - 2.7.6

Enamel on Silver - 5.7.6
" on Silver-gilt 6.2.6

Shagreen, with Silver mounts.
5.10.0

Rosewood, Ivory angled.
3.7.6

Walnut, Ivory angled.
2.17.6

Thuya Wood, Ivory angled.
3.10.0

Crocodile, with Silver-mounted Glass
Ash Tray and Striker.
5.15.0

Oak, Metal-gilt mount.
1.15.0

Tortoiseshell, with Ivory Inlay.
5.15.0

Shagreen, with Ivory Inlay.
4.5.0
Shagreen only. 3.15.0

Tortoiseshell and Brass Buhl.
11.5.0

Chromium Plate, with Onyx Base.
Inlaid Canadian Lapis.
As illustrated.
3.0.0
Plain Onyx Base - 2.7.6

Quartered Walnut, with Metal-gilt Ash Trays.
7.12.6

Chromium Plate, with Shagreen Base.
2.7.6

WRITE for CATALOGUE.

THE 1930s & THE SECOND WORLD WAR

Both Asprey's and Betjemann's suffered as a result of the slump of 1929. The demand for all luxury goods declined, and Asprey's lost some of their American millionaire clients. Asprey's made the best of a bad situation and in about 1930 under the supervision of one of their directors, A.W. Hilling, they started an advertising campaign in *Punch* for which Jacobus Betlem prepared some outstanding colour advertisements. This was a period when *Punch* took no advertisements for liquor. The campaign was a great success, and business gradually picked up. Number 169 New Bond Street was purchased, the remaining part of 22 Albemarle Street was taken over in 1926 and a lift was installed. In 1934 it was decided to build a room as an additional part of 168 New Bond Street, to accommodate an extensive display of Royal Worcester china. This is the room where antique clocks are now displayed.

Eric Asprey's visits to Germany in the 1930s convinced him that a war was inevitable, and he persuaded the directors to start work on a strongroom. This was completed on the day war was declared, bar the painting inside. As an added precaution a second strongroom was taken in Chancery Lane, but this turned out to be a disastrous move, as the safe deposit was bombed and flood water ruined not only the entire stock of watches stored there but also many of Asprey's archives. Eric Asprey recalls:

> At that time we had no other property except our factory at Nettlefold House, Euston Road, and my wife and I, with Mr Hubbard, started to look for accommodation outside London, in case of serious damage to Bond Street. We visited Bath, Harrogate, Chester and Cheltenham, finally deciding on half

a shop in Cheltenham. After the war we were able to acquire the whole building. This turned out to be a very good investment: we later sold it to Austin Reed.

During the war the Nettlefold House factory was managed by W.F. Eve, who headed a group of silversmiths responsible for supplying the Admiralty and other government departments with various parts. This helped the war effort, but was also a boon to Asprey's as it kept together a body of skilled craftsmen who would otherwise have been dispersed to do different war work.

It was during the Second World War that the tact of Mr Hubbard gained for Asprey's one of their most valued clients: Haile Selassie, Emperor of Ethiopia, who had been expelled from his country by the Italians:

> He was over here, living at Brown's Hotel [Mr Hubbard recalled], and he wasn't being treated all that well by some people. He came in here and made a number of purchases and then said, 'Send those to me cash on delivery at Brown's.' I said, 'Nothing of the kind. If you care to take them, you may do so, and the account will follow in due course.' When he got back again, I had an invitation to go out and see him. The first words with which he greeted me as he shook hands were: 'I shall never forget how you treated me when I was more or less an outcast.' Going out there was not just a courtesy trip. It was the forerunner of our opening up abroad, which was so necessary and today of course is going on perfectly.

Another wartime visitor was King Haakon of Norway, who used to come in with his son, Crown Prince Olaf. 'King Olaf comes in now every year during the meeting of the Royal Yacht Squadron,' Mr Hubbard said, 'and in October for his Christmas shopping.'

Another result of the war, when new goods were almost unobtainable and a large second-hand market developed, was the starting of the antique silver department of Asprey's, which was followed soon after the war by antique furniture and interior decoration departments. Immediately after the war, concessions were arranged with the Post Exchange at some of the American bases and exhibitions were staged at horse shows and county

Bond Street showroom, 1939

agricultural shows. Displays were also organized in the Middle East, largely by Mr Hubbard. In 1953 displays were held in Addis Ababa, Jeddah and Baghdad. Long before, Mr Hubbard had described to the Prince Regent of Iraq the work Asprey's had done on Captain Wolf Barnato's house, and the Regent had promised that when the palace in Iraq was built Asprey's would have an opportunity to quote for the furnishings; this finally happened in 1953.

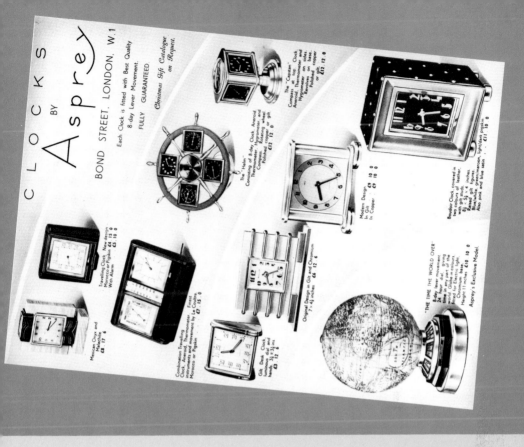
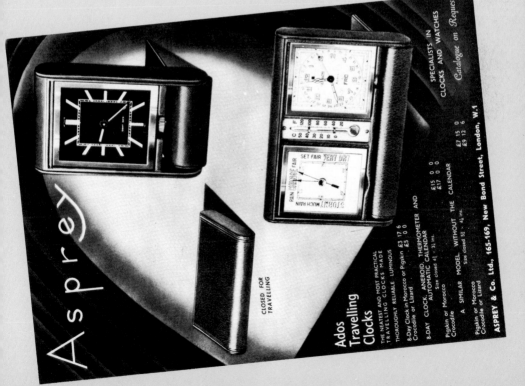

Asprey

ASPREYS NEW WRITING SETS

Smart and neat in appearance, ever lasting in wear. In black Crocodile, black Morocco and Pigskin, stitched on solid Leather, with Chromium roller hinges. The Set illustrated is in Pigskin, and the prices are:—

ALWAYS
SOMETHING
NEW AT
ASPREYS

General Catalogue on Request

Blotter	£7 15 0	Inkstand	£7 15 0
Stationery Case	7 15 0	Memo Pad	2 12 6
Rocker Blotter		Engagement Pad	3 2 6
with Clock	6 15 0	Library Set	3 2 6
		Lamp	£8 10
		Cigarette Box	7 15
		Calendar	1 15

ASPREY & CO. Ltd. 165-169, NEW BOND STREET LONDON, W.1

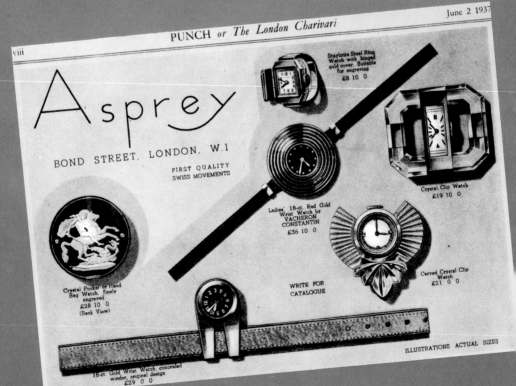

PUNCH *or The London Charivari*

viii

Asprey

BOND STREET, LONDON, W.1

FIRST QUALITY
SWISS MOVEMENTS

Staybrite Steel Ring
Watch with hinged
gold cover. Suitable
for engraving
£8 10 0

Crystal Clip Watch
£19 10 0

Ladies' 18-ct. Red Gold
Wrist Watch by
VACHERON
CONSTANTIN
£36 10 0

Carved Crystal Clip
Watch
£21 0 0

Crystal Pocket or Hand
Bag Watch, finely
engraved
£28 10 0
(Back View)

WRITE FOR
CATALOGUE

18-ct. Gold Wrist Watch, concealed
winder, original design
£29 0 0

ILLUSTRATIONS ACTUAL SIZES

LONDON'S BRILLIANT SEASON

This year's London season is proving the most brilliant and eventful since the war. The Courts will be graced by the personal appearance of the King, now completely restored to health, and already accommodation is being reserved from all over the world by visitors anxious to share in the ever-changing pageant of events.

Never before has the calendar contained so many brilliant and important functions to entertain the unofficial delegates of all nations. The Royal Academy, the Opera at Covent Garden, the Flower Show and Horse Show, Torchlight Tattoo, the Derby, Ascot and Cowes—these are but a few of the brilliant functions that figure in the social round of the coming season.

Brilliant balls will be given by London hostesses, and Charity Dances now being arranged are the Empire Eve Ball, Queen Charlotte's Birthday Ball and the Bal Masqué organised by the Countess of Pembroke in aid of King's College Hospital. The Season will reach its climax with the opening of the Imperial Conference in September, when many brilliant banquets and receptions will be held in honour of the delegates and their wives.

Visits are expected from three future queens—the Crown Princesses of Belgium, Italy and Norway.

Asprey

Cocktail Cabinets

A comprehensive range of cabinets, shakers, glasses, and all cocktail accessories in stock. Special cabinets designed and made to order.

Catalogue on request.

CLOSED

Cocktail wagon, in figured walnut and chromium. Fitted 8 cocktail glasses, 8 tumblers, etc.

£27 · 0 · 0

Elevette fitted with 8 tumblers, and 8 cocktail glasses in non-spill fittings. Automatic closing. In mahogany with chromium mounts. £23 · 10 · 0
In walnut with Chromium mounts £25 · 0 · 0

Limed oak, fitted white footed English glass—large drawer and tray ; automatic lighting inside. £47 · 10 · 0

Figured walnut, with rising back panel fitted English cut glass. Separate serving tray etc. Fitted electric light.

£60 · 0 · 0

ASPREY & Co. Ltd. 165-169, New Bond Street, London, W.1

C.F.H.

Aspreys
E S T A B L I S H E D   1 7 8 1

COCKTAIL CABINETS

A SPREYS have ready in stock a comprehensive range of Cocktail Cabinets of distinctive design, made in every variety of wood. They are also in a position to furnish their customers with attractive sketches for Cocktail Cabinets of special design, embodying customers' own ideas, or harmonising with individual furnishing schemes. Aspreys long experience renders these sketches of considerable value. In addition to Cocktail Cabinets, Aspreys also make a special feature of Glasses, Shakers, and all Cocktail Requisites.

LIMED OAK BARREL with chromium plated bands. Contains 6 English Crystal cut glass tumblers (ASPREYS REGD. BARREL DESIGN) and space for 1 bottle of whisky and syphon. Lift to open. Closes automatically.

Price £25.0.0.

Also a larger size barrel with increased capacity

£35.0.0

Finely figured ENGLISH WALNUT COCKTAIL CABINET fitted with English Crystal glass and 3 chromium mounted glass trays at top.

£80.0.0

ASPREY & COMPANY, LIMITED, 165-169, NEW BOND STREET, LONDON, W.1.

British Craftsmen
NO. 2

The House of Asprey, of Bond Street, London, is well known as a leading supplier of gifts of every description. The exclusiveness and craftsmanship of the articles to be seen in Asprey's salons is due to the organisation of their London factory with its staff of master craftsmen and artists, who still maintain the high standard of workmanship and design which has been the policy of the Asprey direction for generations

Craftsmanship in Gold and Silver

An article which appeared in The Chemist and Druggist, *December 1949*

1. Bond Street, London's leading shopping centre

2. Material selection, cutting out and inspection room

3. Leather craftsmen at work

4. Individual craftsmanship on jewel and fitted cases

5. Final touches to a large jewel case, with lift-out tray

6. Craftsmen engaged on precision production in gold and silver

7. Fine limit lathe and tool work

8. Foreman giving micrometer check-up on prototypes

9. Highly-skilled gold and silver polishers

10. Polishers preparing the work by process of stoneing before engine turning and final polishing

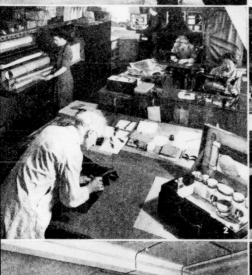

Craftsmanship in Leather

The fuel crisis of February 1947.
Two hundred candles were burnt
a day for two weeks.

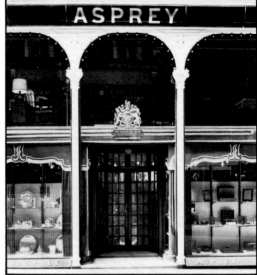

By Appointment

Silversmiths and Jewellers to His Majesty the King

Asprey

Bond Street London

A catalogue cover of the 1950s

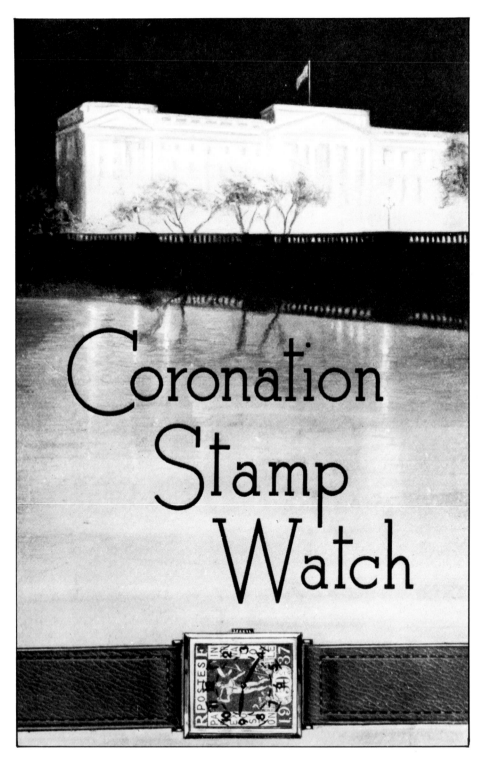

Coronation
Stamp
Watch

*Asprey's in
the 1950s*

The Coronation of our own Queen also took place in 1953. To mark the occasion, Asprey produced a 'Coronation Year Gold Collection', the main part of which was a Coronation dessert, coffee and liqueur service in 18-carat gold, weighing a total of 850 oz. Each piece carried the Coronation Hall Mark, and the set took a year to complete. In producing it, Asprey's wanted to prove that the hand-chaser of 1953 compared favourably with the great masters of the past, especially Paul de Lamerie, once of Bond Street. The collection also included some individual pieces: two 18-carat gold cigar boxes, one of which showed Coronation scenes on a background of lapis lazuli, with an engraving of Westminster Abbey on the lid; two brush sets; a crocodile dressing case with gold fittings; a hand-engraved 'book' pattern cigarette case in four colours of gold; and a crocodile writing set with gold-mounted inkstand and corners. In April 1953 the collection went on show in Bond Street, and was later sent round cities of the United States. The export value of the whole collection was about £50,000 at the 1953 gold rate, that of the dessert, coffee and liqueur set alone being £27,000.

In 1959 Asprey's acquired the old-established firm of Birch and Gaydon at 153 Fenchurch Street, with the object of providing close-at-hand facilities for customers in the City of London with little time to visit the West End. When Asprey's first moved to Bond Street in the 1840s, Henry Gaydon was making watches and chronometers for City men. His son William had been running the firm for sixty years when Asprey's took over, but had no son of his own to continue the business. The Fenchurch Street branch carries a comprehensive stock from the Bond Street showrooms.

In May 1972 Asprey opened their Top Table Room at Bond Street for silver, glass and china. Subsequently the downstairs premises were redeveloped, as was 16 Grafton Street which up to that time had always been let. This building is now connected to Bond Street. The two lower floors are devoted to jewellery, and the upper floors to a board room/dining room. In 1974 a company was opened in Geneva, which now has offices at 40, rue du Rhône.

On 12 April 1975, Asprey's were honoured by the Queen's Award to Industry for outstanding export achievement. They have continued the tradition of shrewd takeovers by acquiring in recent years Lucas, furniture restorers, and Sangorski and Sutcliffe, the famous book binders.

Two examples of pieces made for the Coronation Year Gold Collection. These photographs appeared in The Social Spectator, September 1953.

Asprey

Company Gifts and Presentations

A gift that can be enjoyed *all* the time is a gift in the
truest sense of the word. Nothing better qualifies for this day-by-day
appreciation than a gift of silver, and nowhere can the choice
be more easily made than at Asprey's. This hand-made tea and
coffee service—a fine example of contemporary craftsmanship—
is just one of numerous designs to be seen here amongst a
shining array of silver in all its most elegant forms.

ASPREY & COMPANY LIMITED · 165/169 NEW BOND STREET · LONDON · W.1

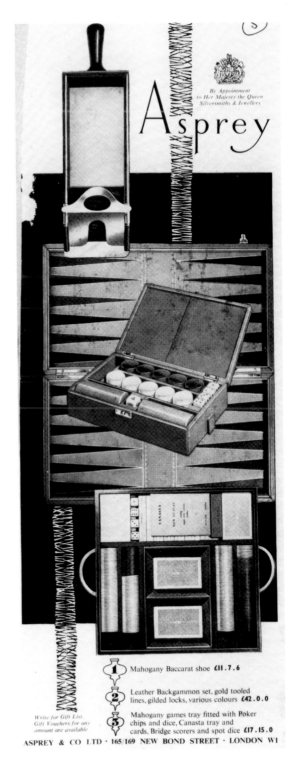

107

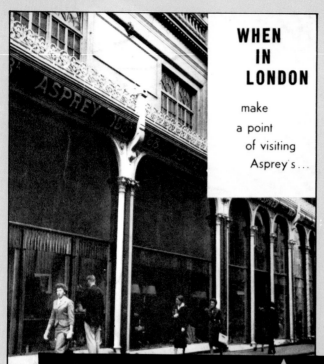

for the art of giving Asprey's stock of cultured pearls is extensive. Single row necklaces from £35.0.0. The three row necklace illustrated has a pearl and diamond clasp price £250.0.0. The black satin covered handbag with gold frame costs £310.0.0. You are invited to send for a copy of the latest illustrated catalogue.

By Appointment to H.M. The Queen Silversmiths & Jewellers

ASPREY IN THE CITY. The City man will find a usefully close-at-hand service at Asprey and Birch & Gaydon, 153 Fenchurch Street where, besides the comprehensive stock held, any pieces can be sent from Bond Street at short notice.

ASPREY & CO. LTD · 165/169 NEW BOND STREET · LONDON W1 · Tel: HYD 6767

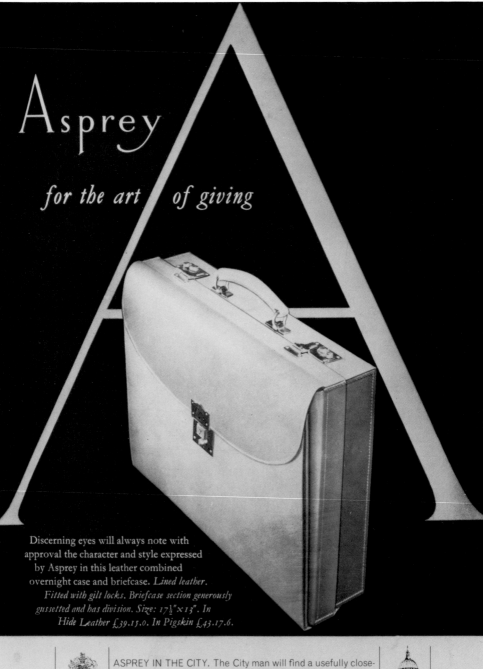

Asprey

for the art of giving

Discerning eyes will always note with
approval the character and style expressed
by Asprey in this leather combined
overnight case and briefcase. *Lined leather.*
Fitted with gilt locks. Briefcase section generously
gussetted and has division. Size: 17½"×13". In
Hide Leather £39.15.0. In Pigskin £43.17.6.

By Appointment to
H.M. The Queen
Silversmiths & Jewellers

ASPREY IN THE CITY. The City man will find a usefully close-
at-hand service at Asprey and Birch & Gaydon, 153 Fenchurch Street where, besides the comprehensive stock held,
any pieces can be sent from Bond Street at short notice.

ASPREY & CO. LTD · 165/169 NEW BOND STREET · LONDON W1 · Tel: HYD 6767

ASPREY TODAY

John Rolls Asprey, 1937 –
Chairman 1979 –

In spite of the aggrandizement of the firm during and since the nineteenth century, Asprey's remains essentially what it was when Charles Asprey set up shop in Bond Street in the 1840s: a family firm specializing in luxury goods. John Asprey (son of Eric) plays a leading part in the company today. Now Chairman, he spent a year in France, a year in Canada with a large jewellery firm and more than a year working in the Swiss watch trade. He is an expert on antique clocks, and also suggests to Asprey's designers the ideas for the magnificent coalitions of gold and precious stones for which there is now such a market in the Arab world: Aztec jadeite stone falcons; jewelled kingfishers catching jewelled fish in their beaks; hummingbird clocks and golden elephants.

The silver and gold work is done in Asprey's factory above the shop, which moved there from Nettlefold House in Euston Road just after the war. Here you might see a Harrier Jump Jet being made with meticulous care to scale – a job which will take the workman a year. Underneath his workbench is a leather apron to catch the gold powder and scraps which are then recycled. Among Asprey's most ambitious productions of this kind have been a model of the *Queen Elizabeth II*; a model of the first floating oil derrick, in gold; and a silver model of Concorde, which has already made a reappearance in Sotheby's auction rooms alongside the antiques whose quality it rivals. Elsewhere, another skilled craftsman is working on a silver cigar box centrepiece with crystal covers; another is working on gold coffee-pot spouts; someone else is making an exact replica of the Derby bell which used to be rung for the start of the Derby, and this will be presented to the owner of the winning Derby horse. Wares are doused in acid-baths, smoothed with pumice-stone and grease mops, gilded in the gilding shop where there is a cyanide solution bath (and cyanide antidote always on hand too). Also in the gilding shop is a big Milner's safe full of gold sheets and silver sheets – and the Ascot Gold Cup in an unfinished state. A casket with a scene of Mecca on top is in preparation. So is a silver world globe, fifty inches in diameter, with the principal cities in precious stones; eventually this will be mounted on a motor-driven stand.

Downstairs, in the Top Table Room, there is Christofle plate from France, exquisite Limoges porcelain, Baccarat glass – including chandeliers and crystal balls for fortune-tellers – and Royal Worcester china. In the luggage department you can still buy Gladstone bags – a misnomer, as the Grand Old Man never used them – and picnic hampers or special luggage that fits snugly into the boot of a Rolls. Asprey's games room is stocked with every kind of backgammon board, including a large folding set with 9-carat gold and sterling silver pieces. Or you can buy a big games compendium in walnut with all-ivory pieces for about £4,000. Luxuries such as leather bindings for telephone directories may be had from the leather department. In the jewellery section, pieces are made from Asprey's own designs. Or there is a superb off-the-peg tiara at £225,000, containing 628 brilliants weighing 166.73 carats, baguettes weighing 15.28 carats and a Burma ruby of 17.35 carats.

Asprey's will go to any lengths to meet a customer's individual requirements. One day a corporation accountant wrote to Mr Eric Asprey and said he wanted a gold toothbrush that would fit into his waistcoat pocket so that he could clean his teeth after business lunches. Mr Asprey summoned the resident designers and put the craftsmen to work. Soon the finished product was on its way to America: a 9-carat gold telescopic handle with a pure bristle brush-head, all reducing to the size of a pill-box. Asprey's put dozens of these collapsible toothbrushes into stock and sold them all.

The firm frequently gets good ideas for merchandise from the quirks and special needs of its customers. On another occasion a man came to them with an armful of expensive shirts; all had collars of different lengths. Was there such a thing as an adjustable collar stiffener? 'Not in stock, sir, but of course we can make them for you.' The collar stiffeners were made – in 9-carat gold. The customer claims they were 'the best investment as a conversation piece that I've ever made'.

Another admirer of Asprey's is a Texan millionaire whose

Mr Eric Asprey receiving the Queen's Award for Industry in 1975

favourite lunchtime snack was a treble-decker sandwich with eggs and a twist of bacon on top. On a visit to his company in Switzerland he complained that no local restaurant could produce a toasted sandwich to satisfy him. The whole issue became rather a joke. Just before his return to the States he received from the Swiss company a treble-decker toasted sandwich with eggs and a twist of bacon–but beautifully made in silver-gilt by Asprey's. The firm's craftsmen had actually toasted three slices of bread in their workshop, fried the eggs, broiled the bacon, assembled the sandwich, made a mould and cast it. The silver-gilt sandwich now sits on the Texan's desk.

From the Mitcham ironmongery of the eighteenth century to such gilded dainties is certainly a big leap, but Charles Asprey's definition of his merchandise in 1851 still holds good under his great-great-great-grandsons: 'articles of exclusive design and high quality, whether for personal adornment or personal accompaniment and to endow with richness and beauty the tables and homes of people of refinement and discernment'.

Two of Asprey's master craftsmen at work

The hallmarks used by Asprey's during 1977, the Queen's Jubilee year

Silver-gilt cup, made each year to be presented at Ascot races

Pair of silver cast chased penguins mounted on an onyx plinth

118

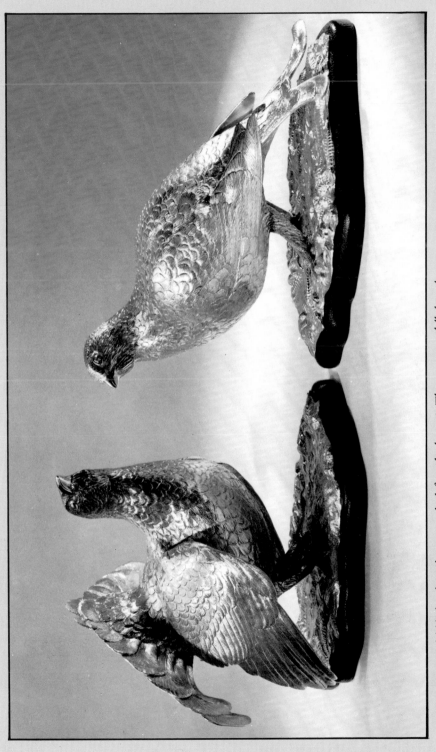

A pair of silver model blackcocks. The one on the left is 'displaying'. These were modelled on the largest pair of blackcocks ever shot in Scotland and were presented to the Gunmakers' Company.

Set of silver-gilt place mats showing different scenes

Eighteen-carat gold rose bowl presented to former President Eisenhower on his golden wedding anniversary. The flowers on the cover are the State flowers of the birthplaces of the former President and Mrs Eisenhower, and the State in which they were married. Engraved around the edges are the twenty-two houses in which the Eisenhowers have lived.

This silver-gilt table piece was made for H.I.M. the Emperor of Ethiopia. In the centre can be seen the Seal of Solomon, an outline of Ethiopia and a portrait of the Emperor. A large diamond is mounted immediately below the portrait. The entire piece is set on a green onyx plinth.

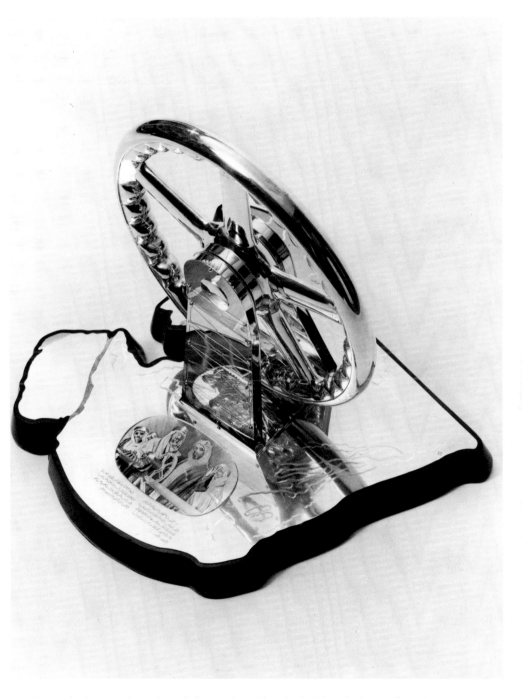

Brass wheel mounted on silver-gilt base with wooden plinth. The wheel came from the customer's oil well. A map of Kuwait and an illustration of the opening of the well is engraved on the base. Made in 1973.

This coffee pot was designed for H.R.H. the Duke of Edinburgh

Specially designed silver racing trophy in the form of an oval dish. A horse and jockey, set on a green onyx base, sit in the centre. One end of the dish is engraved with the Tudor Rose for England, and the other end is engraved with the Rising Sun for Japan. Presented to the Japanese Racing Association by Lord Derby in Tokyo, 1969.

Eighteen-carat gold palm tree. The leaves are made of green gold and garnets are used for the fruit. The tree is mounted on a rose quartz base.

Dessert service in eighteen-carat gold, comprising one oval centre dish, a pair of round dishes, four sweet dishes and a pair of candelabra. Presented to H.I.M. the Shah of Iran on the occasion of his coronation.

A model in silver of the schooner Sir Winston Churchill, *made entirely by hand*

Detail > p. 131

A scale model of a Kuwaiti pearling dhow in silver and silver-gilt. Made for presentation to the Sheikh of Kuwait by the Kuwait Oil Company.

Silver model of a racing car, made in 1973. The special features were taken from the customer's own car.

This model of Concorde took a year to complete. There are approximately 400 assembled parts and several have actually been made to work. The scale is 1/50th of the original and more than 325 ounces of silver were used.

Silver model of the Queen Elizabeth II *made in our Bond Street workshops. The length is 42 inches and weight is 275oz. It consists of approximately 300 pieces and took one craftsman 1,800 hours to complete.*

A Victorian diamond-set tiara of five separate stars set in yellow gold and silver on a white metal frame. Each star is detachable for use as a pendant or a brooch, c. 1860.

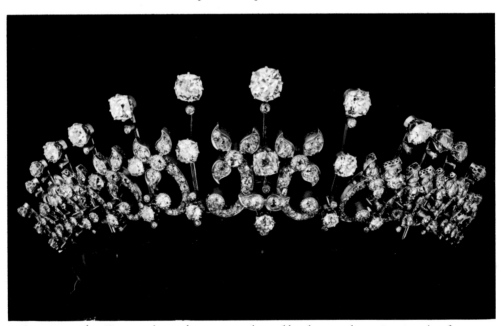

An important late-Victorian diamond tiara set in white gold and mounted on a German silver frame. Made detachable and with a back extension for use as a necklace, c. 1875.

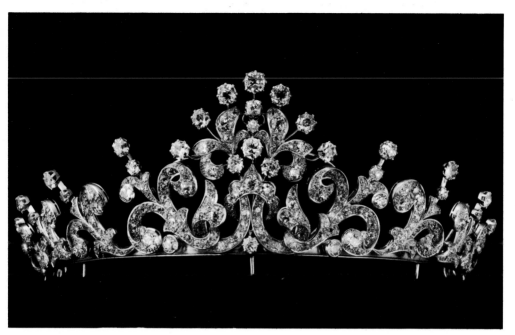

An Edwardian diamond tiara set in white gold and mounted on a German silver frame. Made detachable for use as a necklace, c. 1910.

A magnificent necklace of superb craftsmanship set with brilliant cut diamonds with a detachable cabochon ruby and baguette diamond motif at the centre. The central motif when detached forms a brooch or a pendant at will. The necklace may be worn with or without this motif and is also convertible to a tiara. Designed and made in Asprey's workshop and mounted in platinum.

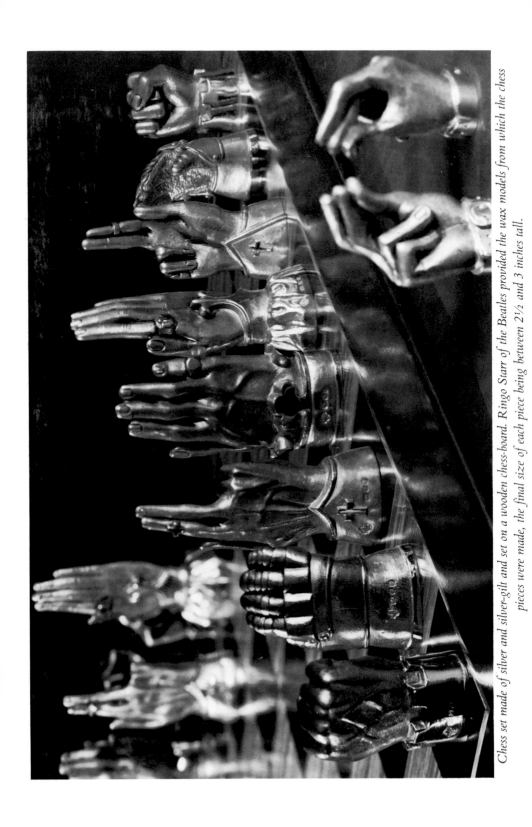

Chess set made of silver and silver-gilt and set on a wooden chess-board. Ringo Starr of the Beatles provided the wax models from which the chess pieces were made, the final size of each piece being between 2½ and 3 inches tall.

This model of the Harrier vertical take-off jet was made by our own craftsmen in silver and silver-gilt.
The scale is approximately 1/20th of the original and took over 2,000 hours to complete.
The length of the model is 28 inches with a wing span of 15 inches.

Fine leathers, rich colours and 200 years of pure craftsmanship. Asprey – for the art of giving.

Established 1781

The Asprey Big Apple

The unique Asprey apple is handmade in 18 carat gold with delicate gold and green enamel leaves. The apple opens to reveal a double photograph frame edged with green enamel and a beautifully designed clock with a matching translucent enamelled face. A tiny gold and scarlet ladybird at the heart of the apple moves to release the photograph frames.

Asprey
BOND STREET LONDON

Asprey and Company Limited, 165-169 New Bond Street, London W1Y 0AR.
Telephone: 01-493 6767. Cables and Telex: 25110 Asprey G.
City Branch, 153 Fenchurch Street, London EC3M 6BB. Telephone: 01-626 2160.
Asprey S.A. Geneva. 40 rue du Rhône, Geneva. Telephone: 28-72-77.

References

1 George Betjeman, who founded the Betjeman cabinet-making business in the early nineteenth century, spelt his surname with one 'n'. In the later nineteenth century, with the popularity of all things German, the name acquired a second 'n'. The present Laureate was born John Betjemann in 1906, but preferred that his surname should revert to the original spelling; the family was Dutch in origin, and the branch from which Sir John is descended came to England in the late eighteenth century.

2 Wilfred Henry Prentis, in *The Snuff Mill Story: Local History of Morden, Mitcham, Merton* (1970) records of Phipps Bridge: 'The "bridge" was two wooden contraptions laid over the two streams of the Wandle. One stream has been filled up and joined to the present grand iron bridge of the "Bailey" type. In about 1769 the Wandle at Phipps Bridge was partially diverted by John Anthony Rucker, a London merchant, to flow into a new "cutt", and a calico printing works was established on the river bank...'

3 Thomas Moore records in his *Life of Byron*: 'During the first months of our acquaintance we frequently dined together alone; and as we had no club in common to resort to – the Alfred being the only one to which he at that time belonged, and I being then a member of none but Watier's – our dinners used to be at the St Alban's, or at his old haunt, Stevens's.' (Stevens's Hotel was at 18 New Bond Street.)

4 The specification of Charles Asprey's patent of handles for dressing cases and despatch-boxes read: 'In all handles hitherto constructed for dispatch and other like cases, they have had the defect of offering too small or uncomfortable a hold. Now, my Invention is intended to remedy this defect, and consists in providing a handle, composed of two flaps or parts, one opposite the other, which, when not required for the purpose of carrying the article, or pulling out a drawer...fold down into hollows or channels made for their reception, and lie flush with that part to which they are fitted...'

5 The author is indebted for this information to research by Miss Betty Masters, Deputy Keeper of the Records, Corporation of London, of the Records Office, Guildhall.

6 On the history of Dee's, see the long footnote by John Culme to Lot 52 in the catalogue of Sotheby Belgravia's sale of 6 November 1975.

7 I am indebted for this and the other facts about Betlem's life to an account by his son, Councillor Pieter Betlem of the London Borough of Hounslow, written at the request of Mr Eric Asprey.

8 See p. 72

8 See p. 72

9 The subscription list opened on 6 July 1909 and closed 8 July 1909. The share capital was £200,000. The average net profits for the years 1906, 1907 and 1908 had been £19,035. This compared with an average net profit for the years 1898, 1899 and 1900 of £7,448.12s 7d. The profit for the twelve months ended 31 March 1921 was £23,368.1s 7d.